TALES FROM
AND

Peter

Illustrated by Sylvia Burgoyne

To Geoff + Sue
Best Wishes
Enjoy
Peter

First published 2019

Front cover photograph by kind permission of
Saint Clements Church Leigh-on-Sea.

ISBN 978-1-5272-3653-0

Contents

These tales I tell are old,
therefore, should be told if wished to last,
beside some flickering fireside nook
as winter mantles a once babbling brook
somewhere in the vales and dales
of our fair Albion.

Foreword

They say that a story is, perhaps, best heard, gathered round the fire, or in the corner of a darkened alehouse. I should know being a storyteller myself and a good friend to Peter Monk. We first met when both of us were performing at Ludlow Medieval Christmas Fayre many years ago; I was telling tales from my tent in the castle and Peter was stilt walking while juggling, joking and bantering with the festive crowds. I became aware that he was loitering close by as I was telling, standing taller than my tent, but bending low, cocking an ear and listening intently to my tales. For it turned out that he too is a storyteller who tells at schools, libraries, art and community centres, places of worship and even in woods and meadows; and as soon as we started talking tales, we hit it off. For Peter and I share a similar taste in stories, also in the way we tell them and just as I have written some books of traditional folk tales, so now has Peter. *Tales from the Shore and More*, the collection of tales you are reading this very day.

Now I know what you're thinking, you started this foreword by saying that stories are best heard and yet this is a collection fixed in print and you'd be right. Moreover, just as that worried me as an oral storyteller when I wrote my first book, so to it must have bothered Peter, for he has made every effort to convey something of the spoken word in his writing, addressing the reader in the first person and commenting on each tale as he tells it, so what follows is a conversation with Peter and it feels as if you are sitting close by him, as he weaves yarns of long ago. So too he employs many a well-honed storytelling trick and technique, using repetition for example to draw the reader into the story, as in 'The Shepherd's Tale,' where he uses it to build humour and also 'The Fisherman's Boy' where conversely, repetition of some of the rhymes helps to build tension.

Like all good storytellers Peter also makes the stories his own, adapting them to his interactive, conversational style, adding humour to soften the darker tales, but balancing the comedy with pathos and thoughtfulness as you'll find out for yourself in tales like 'Arthur and the Butterfly'. The book is also packed full of beautiful phrases, for example when he writes of time, "marching alongside its constant companion, age." Peter's local knowledge also comes into play and his ability to blend his tales with the history of the Thames estuary lends his stories an authenticity. With this book Peter has become so much more than a storyteller and historian, recording other people's stories for posterity, for he is very much part of these stories. Some reflect his own past, being blood-kin to travelers with who he keeps in close contact. He also knows well the various types of boat that sailed from the quay at Leigh-on-Sea long ago and writes of the rusty old ladder there that he himself has climbed many times.

Peter's stories also have a worldly quality, which again relates to his role as an oral storyteller, for the stories he shares have grown in the telling as they have travelled many lands. While some of the stories have their beginnings in Essex, ('The Cutlass Stone,' for example is very much a local tale from Leigh-on-Sea.) his readers must remember that many an Essex sailor, soldier and merchant used the Thames estuary as a starting point for sailing to far flung places long ago, before returning home with many a strange tale from exotic climes; and Peter has done the same, travelling in other lands both as a storyteller and a listener and he provides fascinating insights into the people who originally gifted him the tales in this book as well as the places where first he heard them told. Places like the very end of the snake path at the summit of Masada in Israel.

Some of the stories in Peter's book were already known to me, yet still they surprised me, for he has a way of building the story, painting a picture, drawing the reader into the local landscape. You'll be sure to enjoy his description of Old Father Thames' "gaping mouth" and colourful characters like Churchie Deal and the extremely pompous Ned, both of whom inhabit the same story in this collection. All of which adds to the story to such a degree, that they have been given a new lease of life, with Peter putting such a unique stamp on them, I didn't realise I was reading a story I already knew until the tale was almost read!

Here are stories that span generations of Essex families living beside a small creek on the Thames estuary and beyond and such has been my enjoyment in them that I have already brought two into my own repertoire of tales. Recommendation enough I think of the sheer quality of the tales that Peter Monk has set down below. Silly stories, sad stories and even solemn stories, all of which helps brings a pretty part of long-ago Essex back to life for you the reader. I hope that you enjoy Peter's tales as much as I have.

Dave Tonge
Professional storyteller and author of:
Tudor Tales & Norfolk Folk Tales for Children,
Norwich, October 2018

Acknowledgements

When at school I admit that I wasn't the brightest button in the box when it came to academic subjects as related through the character in the story 'The New Recruit'. My arithmetic was appalling as was my spelling. And as a slow learner (always having a desk at the back of the class as was the general policy in many schools of my era) today it would have been seen that I was possibly somewhat dyslexic and needed some extra help.

However, at one stage of my schooling I had an innovative teacher, Kenneth Hutchinson, who saw potential in my English work that others hadn't. I recall a particular school parents' evening when he was singing my praises about my essays and my Mother saying “But I don't know how you can say that. His spelling is atrocious” “Indeed it is” replied my teacher “but Peter has an imaginative mind. I'm more interested in what he has to say and with him getting it down on the page than if he spells the words correctly. The spelling will come.” Yes, eventually it did come, partly in the form of computer spell check software, but mostly from my good friend of long standing, Richard Mathews to whom I am most grateful for initially proof reading all of my stories.

I also wish to thank fellow storyteller and friend Dave Tong (“The Yarnsmith of Norwich”) himself a published author of two books, 'Tudor Tales' and 'Norfolk Folk Tales for Children', for unselfishly taking the time to cast an experienced professional eye over each one of my stories and for his expert opinion as to their merit for inclusion in the book.

The illustrations in 'Tales from The Shore and More' are from the pen and brush of artist Sylvia Burgoyne. In 1991 I devised a community play for my home town in Leigh-on-Sea. Sylvia whom I had known since about 1973 through my working connections at the Palace Theatre in Westcliff-on-Sea kindly produced an artist's impression of the different scenes at various locations around the town as I depicted them. Those same illustrations became the influence and basic staging format of the Leigh Folk Festival which was kick started by the late Sean Wyre as a contribution to National Music Day in June 1992. The Folk Festival remains a popular annual event and Sylvia's pictures still have pride of place on my stairwell, so it was an obvious choice for me to ask Sylvia if she would be the one to put ink to paper for my first book. Thank you, Sylvia, for agreeing to do so.

I am indebted to Paul McDowell for transcribing the music score.

Thanks go to my wife Gill and my youngest son Tim for putting up with the constant muttering and mumbling to myself as I wandered around the home creating sentences for this or that story.

A special thank you to my son Andrew for his tireless patience with me as I endlessly switched and changed my requirements while he skilfully formatted my work into a book ready document. Without his valuable help and enthusiasm my work would not have seen the printing press, and you my reader, would not have seen this book and the stories within.

Thank you also to Amy Stretch Parker of 'A Spark in the Sand' for her valued advice and help regarding self-publishing.

And lastly a big thank you to all theatres, festivals, schools, fairs, clubs and other organisations who over the many years have engaged me as an oral storyteller or in some other capacity under my stage name Peter Optical.

The Tides Return

I don't want to go said the tide to the shore
it takes me six hours to get here.
From way out there as far can be seen
near to the end of the pier.

Out there I'm ridden by bright colour boats
so I raise up a wave for to thrill.
But I like it here wetting the shore
with sandcastles their moats to fill.

It’s fun to tickle children's feet
when in me they run and play
and just for fun when the wind gets up
I create some waves and spray

Sometimes I'm rough sometimes I'm calm
but still I come back for more
With the help of the moon and a salty breeze
I always come back to the shore.

When it's time to leave I struggle to stay
In temper I swell out then in
and crash on the shore in temper, in rage
But sadly I never win.

I don't want to go said the tide to the shore
it takes me six hours to get here.
From way out there as far can be seen
near to the end of the pier.

Old Mother Moore

The Sea Witch of Old Leigh

There are numerous stories from the old town of Leigh-on-Sea and we who have been brought up or lived in the vicinity of Leigh all our lives, I believe are best placed to tell such tales. Some true. Some not so true and others ....well, it's for you my reader to judge as I relate to you one of many stories concerning Old Mother Moore.

In her younger years Sarah, for that was her Christian name, was a very pretty woman who could turn many a young fisherman's head as he made his way along the cobbled street to one of three wharfs where would be moored, conducive to the local trade, fishing Smacks and Bawleys with their skiff attached which gently swayed from side to side and bobbed up and down as the incoming tide flowed into the muddy tall banked creek.

One sunny day, an hour past noon to be precise, Sarah having already dallied for a while at the cockle sheds also decided to stop off at the forge for a chat. It might have been tiredness or Sarah's unexpected presence which quite understandably might have distracted the young smithy who struck wrongly that fateful hour causing a splinter of white-hot iron to break away from under the hammer's blow upon the anvil and hit young Sarah on the upper lip. Her screams of agony could be heard the length of the cobbled High Street and some say that the gulls as of one accord took flight in startled fluster from where they had contently swum on the tidal waters or roosted on the weather-worn gunnels of fishing boats.

Immediately the poor disfigured young woman hid herself away from prying eyes, in her black painted weather boarded cottage not a stone's throw from the wharf named after the then reigning Monarch.

It was there, in her sparsely furnished home, it is said she discovered, wrapped in sacking on a hidden sooty ledge within the chimney, some old dusty, musty leather-bound books that had belonged to her great grandmother. And from then onwards, often on the night of a full moon when the clock on the tower of St Clements struck the late night hours and the wise bird hooted, Sarah would be seen, although with head and face masked within the hood of her dark cloak, scuttling, as if a rodent, from shadow to shadow past the cockle sheds westwards towards the slopes of the ancient tumbled down castle on the windswept downs.

There she would gather roots and herbs, as were illustrated on the crinkly brown stained pages of the leather-bound volumes. With plants such as Saint John's Wart, and the roots of yellow dock she would make potions and soothing lotions. Some people said that while there on the hill she danced naked in the moon's rays and talked to the hares that bounded about on the grassy slope known locally as the 'Saddleback'.

It was a year to the day from when the accident happened that Sarah was first seen again in daylight by the people of that small fishing community alongside the Thames estuary.

She could still turn the head of a young fisherman but now only to look away from her and at all costs avoid eye contact in an attempt to somehow erase the now embarrassing memory of a kiss under the mistletoe in the snug bar of the Crooked Billet on a Boxing Day morning or a Mayday romp behind a hedge of some local meadow.

Sarah's back was now bent possibly due to rickets. Her hair was thin, grey and matted. Her face pallid for lack of sunlight emphasised the ruddiness of her upper lip, partially split and twisted up into the nostrils which also gave her once dainty nose a hook like appearance resembling that of a characterised fictitious witch.

I take pause here to ask you my reader not to think bad of the people of Leigh for they did not abandon Sarah over the time of herself imposed solitary existence. Their sympathy and offers of help were genuine for they would leave food at her door and jugs of fresh milk as well as churns of cool water that they drew from the nearby well. Some kind person also left, tied outside on the boot scrape, a kitten to keep her company. The whole year the community gave assistance to Sarah and well she remembered their kindness.

Indeed Sarah's appearance, I'm sure from my description, you will agree was no longer attractive to behold and admire. However, respect we must, her warm and kindly personality, her good heart as well as her determination to overcome her misfortune. Having once again ensconced herself back into society the potions and creams that she created from her nocturnal trips to the castle she put to good use for the welfare of all Leigh folk. Some say she had 'swallowed' the ancient books which had equipped her with the knowledge to be a wise woman, a Cunning, a mistress to the 'old craft.'

Back in Sarah's day times were hard. There was no National Health Service and a doctor's fee could often be unaffordable to the majority of families by the waterside. Therefore, people like Sarah were treasured for the administering of her various cures to the sick as well as being skilled in the practice of midwifery. There remain to this day, many in the Old Town who can trace their ancestors to having been brought into this world by Sarah; later to be known as Old Mother More.

Naturally she wasn't liked by everyone in that small hamlet at the water's edge especially by the more ardent Christian folk who attended the small nearby chapel or made the steep climb up the worn steps to the church at the top of the hill. Yes, the gossipers and rumour mongers were always ready to dream up a yarn or two to discredit Mother Moore especially in her later years. Now old and wrinkled by the salt sea air she was the target of malicious mischief makers who accused her of being a witch, being in league with the devil and her black cat, left as a kitten by an unnamed well-wisher, now her familiar.

Some told how they had been cursed or knew of someone who knew someone, who knew someone else who had been cursed. However, the majority of the people had no axe to grind and would often seek advice from her which often involved the telling of fortunes through the sprinkling of fine sand on water or reading the palm. It's true that Old Mother Moore, partly due to her age, would get irritated by this or that the same as we all can. Children being particularly loud and playing two ball or three ball up against the wall of her cottage or endlessly rolling iron hoops backwards and forwards under her window could indeed try her patience and she would come out and chase them off with some rough words while brandishing a besom broom. That aside on the whole and to her credit she wasn't aggressive except only if truly offended; then, well... it's best you read on.

On sunny days with her cat at her feet she would sit in her old rocking chair on Bell Wharf smoking her clay pipe gazing out to sea and if anyone should come by to untie and cast off their boat onto a rising tide Old Mother Moore would abruptly put out her hand and say “Coin for fine weather” This meant that if you gave Sarah some money then she would guarantee you a fair wind and a safe passage on the deep salt sea.

There was a certain amount of superstition among the fishermen of Sarah Moore's era so some would pass over a coin in the belief that she could control wind and tide.

Others just quietly and politely humoured her and gave her a coin anyway... or maybe just in case.

One fine day, a Friday to be exact, with only the slightest of a breeze to ruffle a boat's brown canvas sail and with the estuary's water a deep turquoise under a cloudless sky and as tranquil as a mill pond there on the wharf sat Old Mother Moore like I have already described when surprisingly, being that particular day of the week, a small vessel arrived from across the water in Kent. If its three-man crew were Men from Kent or Kentish men due to whatever side of the River Medway they had been born is of no consequence. But having climbed the thirteen rusty rungs of the rusty iron ladder, which many a time I myself have climbed on to the quayside they were confronted by Old Mother Moore. "Coin for fine weather gentlemen" she politely asked "Away with you, you dirty old bag of foul-smelling rags. You'll get nothing from us" they jeered then spat and kicked the cat before making their way down the small narrow cobblestoned high street to buy provisions and take refreshment at one or two of the many hostelries that lined the narrow pavement.

On their return to the wharf in readiness to set sail, again Sarah stuck out her bony hand and politely suggested that they might like to give her a coin for fine weather and once more those three men hurled abuse at her with words that I fear would taint this page.

Back down the rusty iron ladder they went laughing and joking at the expense of the old lady sitting in her rocking chair smoking her clay pipe. However, if even just one of those obnoxious three had bothered to have given Sarah the slightest of glances before she disappeared from their view as they descended down the ladder onto the deck of their clinker built boat they would have seen that Old Mother Moore's eyes had turned a deep fiery red, the colour of the Smithy's bellowed forge and to see such would have put abject fear into their black hearts.

With their supplies stored below deck they hoisted the canvas sail, untied the boat from its mooring and pushed off from the wharf. Following the course of the creek's current they slowly drifted out into deeper water while Mother Moore in her chair increased her rocking. Rocking, rocking backwards forwards backwards forwards faster and faster she went until the tiny boat was far out in the deep water of the Ray then Sarah gave a screech as loud as that of a thousand seabirds and instantly the summer breeze turned into a gale as the sky turned dark with thunder clouds while the water seemed to bubble like a witches cauldron then rose up as gigantic waves. One minute the tiny craft would be riding high the awesome crest and the next, deep down low in the waves trough it would go to be surrounded on all sides by a wall of grey cold salt sea water. While all the time out there off shore the storm raged; on Bell Wharf under a blue sky and in bright sunlight Old Mother Moore watched the storm raging in the estuary as she kept rocking, rocking backwards, forwards backwards and forwards.

Out on the turbulent water the captain or whatever he had deemed to title himself yelled above the gale "It's that old crone back on the wharf she's a bloody sea witch. It's she who has gathered up this storm. Go below, get the axe and cut down the mast, release the sail or else it will be the sea's bed for us tonight should we capsize."

One of the crew bravely slid himself across the wave lashed deck and scrambled through the hatch in a volley of water. On his return, with his companions holding his ankles for support he wielded the axe striking hard and furious at the mast ...not once, not twice but three times he struck then with what above the roar of storm sounded like a howl of agonizing pain, the mast, snapped, toppled and fell into the sea taking with it the wind tattered sail.

At that very instant the storm abated and again the sky was cloudless and the sea as tranquil as a mill pond. Without sail the storm drenched exhausted crew had no alternative but to row back to Leigh and the sunlit wharf they had sailed from.

When at long last they arrived the three bedraggled men slowly climbed the thirteen rusty rungs of the rusty iron ladder onto firm ground.

Sarah was still there in her chair, but she was no longer rocking for she was slumped forward with her clay pipe broken in two at her feet which still smouldered like a doused blacksmith's fire. Old Mother Moore was dead.

From three deep wounds to her shoulders and neck, each wound the size of an axe's head, blood found its way across her age-lined cheek to splatter drop by incessant drop from her misshapen lip onto the hard-cobblestoned wharf as the church clock struck the thirteenth hour.

If ever you my reader are intent to go on the waters and someone should ask you for 'a coin for fine weather'... believe what you will.

The Gypsy and the Priest

Although it happened a long time ago, on cold windy nights it is still often talked about in front of a blazing hearth in the snug at the Flying Horse in the small village of Fellwell by the Sea.

The tale starts when a small family of travellers arrived in their horse drawn bow-top caravan and set up a small camp beside the old country lane just along from Worthy Farm. The majority of residents of Fellwell weren't at all perturbed by their new neighbours and were happy to have them around, adding to the rustic charm of the area. Although at times the two children could look a little grubby, but no more so than many other children, they were always polite.

However, there was one person in Fellwell who took an instant dislike to the arrival of the Gypsy family, and that was the Rev Gorger, incumbent of St Christopher's, the parish Church. In no time at all he was able to obtain a court order ruling that the travellers were to vacate their camp in the lane and move on. This they adhered to but only as far as to a field on the farm with the full permission and blessing of its owner. Here Franks horse's, three in all, could shake their manes in the wind and run free. In return Frank, never being workshy did odd jobs and seasonal work at the farm while his wife Maria tended to the family's domestic needs and in the evenings carved dolly pegs out of willow gathered on the banks of a nearby stream. These pegs she sold along with small bunches of heather not only to the villagers of Fellwell but also to those in the nearby village of Overcliff.

To this very day it's still not fully understood as to why so much hatred dwelt and festered in the heart of the Rev Gorger, this said man of the cloth, this man of Holy Orders, but as time passed he became more and more obsessively fearful of the third eye, the sixth sense of a gypsy; those same gifts that Frank was said to possess; intuition, wisdom and the ability to see through a person and beyond and in doing so instantly unravel the fake from the genuine in someone's personality.

Alcoholic beverages (of which the priest was frequently seen to partake) did nothing to quell his dislike of Frank; in fact, such quantities of liquor only served to increase the priest's loathing. Oh yes, drink he did, but was not known to buy a round for he was as miserly as they come. It was said by some the Sunday offertory helped subsidise his drinking habit.

Anyway, to be fair to you the reader, for fear of losing your attention, I will dwell no longer on such details except only to say, be he drunk or sober he would bewail Frank and his family when and wherever he could. Even his Sunday sermons would ridicule and hold in contempt the ways of gypsy folk.

Time, never faltering, as ever marched on alongside its constant companion.... age; and having eventually lost his driving licence somewhere down the plastic tube of a breathalyser the Rev Gorger found it more and more tiresome to visit his parishioners by foot and, if required, offer communion to those who for whatever reason were unable to attend the quaint country church.

One day after a not very sober attempt to master the skills of cycling in a reasonably straight line and on the correct side of the road our Gypsy antagonist decided he would acquire a horse for his travels. After some local enquiries, to his utter dismay, it became quite apparent that the only horses in the area were at Worthy Farm and they were owned by Frank, and even then, it was not known if one would be for sale - especially to somebody who despised and had so much hatred in his heart for their owner.

However, as darkness fell, with a Bible clutched firmly in his hand the Reverend Gorger left the Flying Horse pub with as little staggering as he could muster and made his way up to the farm.

When he eventually arrived, he found Frank and his wife sat at an open fire. "I'm just about to take the kettle off the boil, would you like a cuppa" she said smiling. "Nettle tea alright?" Gruffly the visitor declined for fear of it being drugged, or worse still laced with a deadly poison extracted from some toxic plant or fungi.

Frank slowly poked the fire with a willow stick and watched the sparks flit and dance as they rose up to embrace the night sky. Then holding up the charred withy he said, "Did you know the willow tree has no heart and it was the child Jesus who made it so." "Blasphemy" retorted the uninvited guest "I've not come to hear such profane uttering's which are best kept to yourself and your kind. I'm here to see if…" "I would sell you a horse" said Frank interrupting the Priest in mid-sentence. "You are indeed possessed, in league with the devil" cried the priest clutching his Bible closer to his chest "It's that third eye you have, you steal people's thoughts-for how else would you have known I wanted a horse?" "That was easy" replied Frank. "Before you came up the lane I bumped into Jack from the farm. He'd just been down the Pub and had overheard you say you were looking for someone to sell him a horse. That ain't nothing to do with no third eye, that ain't, that's just putting two and two together and making four."

"Well, will you sell me a horse"? demanded the Priest. "Of course I will. Come with me and you can choose which one you'd like" said Frank giving the fire one last poke.

Revered Gorger followed Frank to the stable which had been kindly provided by farmer Jack when Frank and his family had first moved onto the farm.

"There you are" said Frank as he led his three horses out into the moon lit paddock "The choice is yours" "How much each are they?" enquired the priest, ever minded of cost. "All depends which one you want" replied Frank. The Revered Gorger produced a hip flask from his jacket pocket, took a long swig of its contents and pointed to the dapple grey. "That one there" he spluttered.

"Three hundred guineas" said Frank. "What!" exclaimed the other. "Far too much, what about the brown one?" "The Palomino, two hundred guineas and a bargain at that" assured its owner.

Swallowing the remaining contents of the flask and returning it to his pocket the priest gave one almighty belch, flopped down on a hay bale and retorted "Do you think I'm made of money... what about that black one, looks about ready for the knackers' yard to me… how much for that one?" "To you Sir," said Frank leading the horses back under cover. "One hundred guineas including saddle and all other tack. Take it or leave it"

"I'll take it" quickly snapped the priest, believing he had cleverly outwitted the gypsy because the horse he was about to buy so cheaply was the finest of the three; a true thorough- bred and what with the tack he'd got a fine deal. He had long ago been a parish priest in Newmarket, and he knew a good horse when he saw one, even through a drink induced haze.

Having counted out the money into Frank's work-hardened hands and saddled and reined up the stallion, Reverend Gorger clumsily mounted and urged the horse to walk on.

However, it did nothing of the sort, it just stood there. No matter what the Priest said, whatever he did the horse refused to move.

"What's the matter with this beast" demanded the Priest. "It just stands here and won't budge."

"Ah" said Frank "that's about right, it only moves when it hears the magic word." "Magic word!" exclaimed the frustrated clergyman "May the good Lord forgive you I'll not use any magic word"

"Then you are going to be here a very long time" said Frank "I'm off to my bed, Maria douse the fire will you, it's time to turn in" he shouted as he closed and locked the stable door.

"Very well", said the new owner of the horse, "May God forgive me, what's the magic word?"

"That will cost you, the magic word is extra" said Frank with a wry smile on his lips. "Then how much?" snarled the priest having now realised he was mounted on a black steed as dark as the darkest of nights he thought he had bought cheaply but which refused to move then or anytime in the future.

"One hundred guineas" said Frank. "But that's what I paid for the horse' retorted the other." Take it or leave it, it could be a long dark night" chuckled Frank as clouds gathered to cover the moon.

The Reverend reluctantly agreed the price and handed it to Frank who in turn blew softly and whispered in the horse's ear and then said "Hallelujah" at which the black stallion started to walk, then trot, then gallop round and round the paddock. Faster and faster it went charging round with the holy man desperately tugging on the reign and eventually clinging on to its neck for dear life.

"How do you make it slow down, bring it to a halt" yelled the priest. "Oh, that will be the other magic word" yelled back Frank as the horse and rider galloped past. "And what's that" shrieked, the by now, terrified priest. "It will cost you another hundred guineas I'm afraid" said Frank while trying his utmost to contain his amusement. "Very well" screamed the Reverend Gorger, "Here it is" and he hastily threw down a purse which he at the same time assured Frank contained another hundred guineas.

Frank shouted "Amen" and the black mount whinnied and, in an instant, came to a halt.

"There you have it" said Frank "Now be on your way, your business here is done. One horse, and its two magic words Hallelujah to move and Amen to stop. I bid you goodnight."

Without another word to Frank the Revered Gorger now having gathered his breath and his nerve held tightly the reigns and whispered the word Hallelujah. The horse slowly trotted out of the paddock and down the lane. It soon dawned on the Priest that the overall reaction pace of the horse was controlled at all times by those two words Hallelujah and Amen and had nothing whatsoever to do with magic.

With this new-found confidence in the mastering of his new acquisition he eventually arrived back at the Pub where he bought more than a few drinks for himself and availed upon the landlord to top up his flask.

Then he was again out into the night and after several painful attempts he was once more in the saddle and on his way out of the village past the church of St Christopher to visit the holstery in Overcliff.

I think it safe to presume that it was due to the amount of alcohol that the Reverend Gorger had already consumed and that of further intoxicating liquor in Overcliff that utterly confused his mind as to which direction he should have journeyed to eventually arrive home to the safety of his bed. Not only that, his pickled mind caused him to temporarily forget the magic word for bringing the galloping stallion to a halt before both he and the black horse reached the top of the cliff. Desperately he tried to remember, to remember the word as faster and faster he travelled towards the cliff's edge.

Then, in the very nick of time he remembered and shouted "Amen" at which with hooves digging deep into the turf the horse came to an abrupt holt.

Shaking and sweating but with a great sense of relief the Reverend Gorger crossed himself, raised his arms in thanksgiving and looking up to the clouded heavens yelled at the top of his voice "Hallelujah."

The horse's movement was instant.

It was with the dawn, as the sun was peeping over the ebb tide, the Clergyman was found dead on the wet ragged rocks below the cliff and in the pocket where he was known to keep his flask, they found no such item, other than a small bunch of heather... lucky for some, but not everyone.

That same morning, in the stable, back at Worthy farm there were again three horses, a dapple grey, a Palomino and one as black as the darkest of nights.

This is my slant and twist on the idea of a story I believe I first heard part of long ago in a pub in West Hanningfield Essex.) I myself being of gypsy stock I decided to give it that connection.

When our two boys, Andrew and Timothy were young my wife and I took them for a trip to London. While walking through and along with the crowds in Leicester Square I was just ahead of the other three when I was approached by a woman who was selling small bunches of heather. "Lucky heather Sir" she said while offering a scraggily and seemingly wilting plant right under my nose. "No thank you" I politely replied. Then from behind I heard Andrew the eldest of the two boys say to the woman "I think my dad has more right to sell that than you have."

The Giant of Gosfield

For what reason they had fallen out with each other neither I or anyone else is any the wiser and if the truth be known the two aggrieved persons in my story could well have forgotten how their dislike for each other had begun in the first place. Arguments and disagreements are sometimes like that, they go on and on for so long we often forget how and for what reason they first started.

To be fair, the Mayor of Chelmsford in Essex was willing to forgive and forget, what he had in this case forgotten, and to let bygones be bygones but his antagonist the Giant of Gosfield, a few miles north in the same county, was certainly not willing to do so.

To the people of Chelmsford, the giant at home in Gosfield, stamping around cursing and swearing trying to think of a way to harm their Town Mayor sounded like the rumbling of distant thunder. In fact, many town folk were heard to say, "Sounds like it's going to rain" and although the sky was blue and not a cloud to be seen many rushed to get their umbrellas.

"I know what I will do" said the giant to himself and he grabbed his huge shovel and dug deep in the ground and raised up a huge pile of earth on its blade leaving, there in Gosfield, a massive 36-acre hole in the ground. Now that's one big hole; and having been dug by a Giant it would be wouldn't it!

"With this earth" he angrily muttered to himself "I'm going to go back to Chelmsford and put it into the river that flows through the town, so that it floods and drowns the

Mayor and all the people living there." Then, without further ado off he set for the Chelmer, for that was the name of the river.

Well, the giant with his huge shovel full of earth hadn't gone very far when he decided to rest for a while. After all, even for a Giant a huge shovel full of earth can be very heavy. Sitting down under the blue cloudless sky he soon fell asleep.

Now, those who live in the not too hilly county of Essex know how quickly the weather can change and how fast and silently a thick mist can roll in from the sea and cover the land. As it did so while the Giant slept. When eventually he awoke, he couldn't see his finger in front of his nose. In fact, the mist was so thick he couldn't even see his nose.

Being a giant and by standing up he thought he might be able to see above the mist, but the damp cloud went even higher than him and was just as thick. With his huge shovel and its enormous amount of earth the Giant started walking this way then that way getting himself completely disorientated; totally and utterly lost. He walked and he walked and he walked, then, all of a sudden, the mist lifted and disappeared as quickly as it had come and there was the Giant not knowing where he was or which way to go. It had by now been a long time since he had set off from his home in Gosfield and it was starting to get dark when along the road, whistling a merry tune came a man with a sack on his back. "Oy you" said the giant rudely looking down at the man. "Where am I? I got lost in the mist so which way is it to Chelmsford and how far is it?"

"It's that way" said the man pointing back over his shoulder from the way he had come. "And I said how far is it bellowed the giant. I'm tired from walking around with this massive shovel full of earth." "Why do you walk around with it then" said the man not being at all scared of a giant because he had met many before on his travels especially in Ireland, Wales and Cornwall.

"It ain't none of your business but I'll tell you anyway" retorted the Giant. "I don't like the Mayor of Chelmsford so I'm going to put this earth in the river just beyond that town so it makes a dam and then the river will flood and drown the Mayor and all the people. So how far is it?"

The man who stood looking up at the Giant didn't like the sound of what the giant had to say for he was a cobbler, a maker and mender of boots and shoes by trade and he knew the Mayor and many of the people of that town for it was them that gave him work.

"Well", said the Cobbler thinking hard as to how he could save the Mayor and people of Chelmsford from getting their feet wet and eventually drowning "I've just come from there and it's this far" he continued to say as he emptied his sack onto the road and out tumbled boots and shoes and the odd dog lead. "You see these shoes and these boots, look everyone has a hole in the sole or the heels are worn down and all these boots and shoes are mine (which in a way they were while he mended them) and these boots I have on are also wearing very thin. Chelmsford is so far that I was in fear I would have to finish my long journey here, back home in bare feet."

"Oh no" exclaimed the giant who, wasn't so to speak, the brightest button in the box. "I've only got this one pair of boots. They won't last the journey I've already been walking round and round, this way and that way for hours in the mist and this shovel of earth is getting to heavy even for me. I'm going home." "You live in Gosfield don't you" said the Cobbler while putting the shoes, boots and dog lead or two back in his sack. "What of it" replied the Giant angrily. "Well" continued the knowledgeable cobbler. "If you go back in the direction I have come, then you will reach Gosfield which is long before you would have reached Chelmsford. You have been going completely in the wrong direction. You are now in Hedingham which is north from Gosfield."

And with those words ringing in his ears the Giant threw down the massive pile of earth where he was. Then with the shovel over his shoulder without a word of thanks or bye your leave he stormed off through the darkness towards Gosfield just as it started to rain; and rain it did, it absolutely poured. It bucketed down and there wasn't a cat or dog in sight for they had run for cover not that he would have seen them in the now dark of night.

On arriving back home to Gosfield what with the darkness of that night and the wind and rain in his face beating on his skin like a thousand shoemakers needles the Giant forgot and didn't see the massive 36-acre hole he had dug earlier which was now filled to the very top with water and starting to overflow.

Splash and in he went. His cries for help, for he could not swim, were lost in the high-pitched howling of the uncompassionate wind and very soon he drowned, sinking to the very bottom of what had become a lake; Gosfield Lake. And it is said that if you should go there on a dark stormy night you can hear the giant's mournful cries for help in the voice of the wind through the reeds and feel his tears of remorse in the spray from off the water.

And what of that pile of earth he left at Hedingham! Well, eventually the mound became fertile with lush green grass strewn with small dainty wild flowers and a chap called Aubrey de Vere came along and built a Castle on it and part of that castle remains standing tall to this very day but not quite as tall as was the giant of Gosfield.

But what of the Cobbler; you might well ask! Well, he told his story of his encounter with the Giant of Gosfield to those who could be bothered to listen, but nobody believed him. Still, it's like that sometimes when you tell a story. However, he was happy, much contented whistling a merry tune as he went about his business keeping the Mayor and good people of Chelmsford happily well-shod and dry footed for many a year.

I have heard a similar tale to this from Shropshire. However, this is my slant on that story and being an Essex man born and bred I decided to set it in my home county.

The White Knight

The river is flowing, flowing, flowing
The wind is blowing gently through the reed.

Early each morning just as the suns first rays made sparkle the ripples on the water a young boy named Raglin would go down to the river, the source of which was in a mystical land deep in the earth far, far, away behind Moran Tor and the high dark mountains of Eslip.

The boy's mother would often say "One day the river will swallow you." but Raglin didn't listen and would just give a broad smile, kiss his mother's troubled brow, pick up his flute and make his way silently down the winding track to the water's edge. There he would sit leaning his back against an old willow tree and play.

His tunes sounded so melodious they helped make the river flow, the reeds to grow through which the wind would gently blow.

One morning a young girl, out gathering mushrooms, on hearing the beautiful tunes floating on the breeze, ventured across the buttercup meadow, to find out where the sweet music was coming from and found herself on the opposite bank of the river to where Raglin was sitting playing, his young supple fingers one by one delicately bending and shaping each note on his flute into a haunting melody. So wonderful was the young boy's playing, lifting into the cool clear morning air, that even the lark high on the wing ceased its song to listen.

The girl sat and watched small fishes leap from the fresh sparkling water as if dancing to the enchanting tunes Raglin was playing.

It wasn't long before Raglin was aware she was there. Her beauty immediately snatched his breath away causing him to miss a note. She smiled, her eyes were dark, like the deepest of secret pools, and her hair, raven black, cascaded down to her slim waist. The early morning sun shining on her head gave the appearance of a crown.

Raglin fell in love with her straight away. Never had he seen anyone so beautiful and he played his flute with an even greater passion sending each note across the water as if it were an arrow from Cupid's bow, an arrow of love to gently pierce her heart.

Each morning after, when Raglin went to the river to play his flute, the girl whose eyes were dark, like the deepest of secret pools, and whose raven black hair cascaded down to her slim waist, was there sitting on the opposite bank listening as he bent and shaped each note which made the river flow, the reeds to grow through which the wind would gentle blow. But never did they speak. Not one word passed between them; it was as though his music and her smile said all that was needed to be said. For days, for weeks, for months, they met like this divided by the river and neither spoke a word to the other.

Then one morning Raglin kissed his mother goodbye and was out of the door before she had a chance to say, as she always did, "One day the river will swallow you." and with joy in his heart he ran down the winding track to the river, for this day he would speak to the girl with the dark eyes, and raven black hair. He would tell of his love for her and ask her to marry him.

Leaning his back against the old willow he played his flute to help make the river flow, the reeds to grow through which the wind would gently blow. There he waited while shaping and bending each note as he purposely sent them with all his love across the river towards the buttercup meadow from where would come the love of his life.

But she did not come that day, or the next day or the day following that. Saddened Raglin gave up going down to the river with his flute to help make the river flow, the reeds to grow through which the wind would gently blow but he never forgot or lost his love for the girl with the dark eyes, and raven black hair.

The years passed by and then one day there was a knock on Raglin's door. Standing there was a strangely dressed little man, who was no taller than seven glass bottles of milk on top of each other. He was wearing a gold top hat and reported that there was going to be a big celebration in the town on the other side of the river and would Raglin like to come the following day and play his flute for the dancing in honour of the King's Birthday.

Raglin was happy to agree because apart from the enjoyment of playing his flute it was also a great privilege and honour to be asked to play on such a special day.

Early next morning Raglin said goodbye to his mother, gave her a kiss and told her that before crossing the bridge on his way to the town he would stop off at the old willow by the water's edge and quickly practice some tunes." Be careful" she said, "or one day the river will swallow you." Raglin smiled sadly, for she was getting old, picked up his flute and made his way silently down the winding track to the water's edge.

Leaning his back against the old willow and starting to play, he looked longingly across the water towards the buttercup meadow as he bent and shaped each note to help make the river flow, the reeds grow through which the wind would gentle blow.

When he eventually crossed the old stone bridge that carried the road to the town, he sensed that he was being watched. He stopped. But looking about him, he could see nobody so he continued his journey and was soon amongst a happy throng of townspeople ready to dance and celebrate their monarch's Birthday.

Raglin took out his flute and started to play and they danced and danced until someone shouted, “Look here he comes.” "Who?" enquired Raglin. “The King” came the reply and they all stopped dancing and rushed forward to line the road to see His Majesty come past in his gold carriage drawn by six white horses. That's odd thought Raglin, the strangely dressed little man, who had worn a gold top hat but was no taller than seven glass bottles of milk each on top of the other had said nothing about the King actually coming to the town as part of his birthday celebrations.

However, Raglin had never seen the King before and stood on tip toe and craned his neck to see over the top of the crowd who were now waving flags and cheering as the carriage approached and then stopped for a brief moment right opposite where Raglin stood. There in full view was the King joyfully waving back at the crowd and sitting with him was his daughter. Her eyes were dark, like the deepest of secret pools, and her hair raven black, cascaded down to her slim waist. Raglin's heart skipped a beat then pounded with such fervour as if trying to break free from his chest. It was her, the girl from the river, now a young woman; a beautiful Princess.

With sadness in his heart he turned and walked away. The love of his life, a Princess, how could she ever love him he thought. Him just a young man who played a flute.

With the sounds of cheering and laughter ringing in his ears as if mocking his plight, he started to cross back over the old stone bridge to his own familiar side of the river when who should appear but the strangely dressed little man in the gold top hat who was now no taller than six glass bottles of milk on top of each other.

"You look sad" he said, "Can I help you?" "I don't believe you can. I don't believe anyone can." Raglin replied now anxious to get home and to be as far away from the town as he possibly could. "Try me" said the little man in a voice that sounded somewhat snappier than it had been. So Raglin told the little man, who was now no taller than five glass bottles of milk on top of each other, all about the river, how he would play his flute which helped make the river flow, the reeds to grow through which the wind would gentle blow. And he told him of the girl with the dark eyes, like the deepest of secret pools, and her raven black hair that cascaded down to her slim waist; of how he had fallen in love with her and of the day he was going to ask her to marry him. That day he went to the river and she was not there or ever there again and how he had never set eyes on her beauty since... until a few moments ago when he saw her in the Royal Carriage, as the princess sitting next to her father the King.

"I wish I could change myself be someone else, someone she would admire and fall in love with. But as I am, what chance do I stand?" said Raglin "To her, as a princess, if she should see me like I am, she would see nothing more than a boy, a boy with a flute who she used to watch across a river; that's if she would even recognize me. For like her I am now older. I wish I was a brave knight clad in white armour brandishing a mighty sword that can only be drawn from its scabbard to fight injustice. I wish I had a fine white horse, and that I owned a castle and lands by the ocean where floated a fleet of fine ships that would unfurl their sails and put to sea anytime at my command. I wish I owned gold, silver and precious jewels that sparkle like a kingfisher as it fleetingly skims the water's surface in the early morning sun. Then I would be as rich as a prince, as rich as a King in a position to ask the princess to be my wife."

"All that can be yours for I have the power to make you into that brave knight clad in white armour you so wish to be but if I do that's how you will remain. You can never change back again; for all memory will be erased so be careful what you wish." said the little man removing his gold top hat with a flourish and bowing so low that his nose touched the ground which wasn't that difficult to do considering he was now no taller than four glass bottles of milk on top of each other.

"You can, you really can do that?" enquired Raglin. "Oh yes indeed I can" said the man, who was now no taller than three glass bottles of milk on top of the each other "but it will cost you your flute" he continued to say as he straightened up from his low bow. "Willingly" replied Raglin without the slightest thought or hesitation "Here take it, it's yours" and hurriedly he handed the flute to the man who with or without his gold top hat was now no taller than two glass bottles of milk on top of each other.

"A brave Knight clad in white armour on a fine white horse will have no need of a silly flute" boasted Raglin. The little man, now no taller than one glass bottle of milk, on taking the flute, held it behind his back and out of the sight of Raglin he let it slip silently through a gap between the stones of the old bridge into the river below. Without splash or ripple it entered the cool clear water. Deep it went among the fishes who with a flip of their silvery tails aided it back to the sun kissed surface. The lark high on the wing ceaselessly sung its song as it watched the discarded instrument float on the river's gentle current until it lodged silently among the reeds opposite the old willow tree. "Follow the river to the north, follow it to its source" came the faint squeaky voice of the now teeny, weenie tiny speck of a man as unseen he drowned on the side of the road in a pool of creamy white milk just before, a stray black cat, flicking its tail while purring, delightedly licked it all up.

Having looked round in vain for the whereabouts of the little man and having kicked some broken glass neatly, tidily into the gutter Raglin left the bridge; and he walked and he walked and he walked until eventually he disappeared into a glowing mist at the rivers source deep in the earth behind Maron Tor and the high dark mountains of Eslip and he was never seen again.

That could have been the end of my story. The book could have been closed or the storyteller, having been paid a moderate fee, could have gone home; and you the reader, you the listener could have retired to your bed and given yourself over to dream-spin your own tales.

However, season followed season. The year turned around again, again and again and all remained at peace in that little Kingdom where the Princess lived. Her father the King was a good, just man who ruled wisely and was dearly loved by the people.

But one day an evil, greedy King from a neighbouring country, wanting to divert and alone have possession of the river, amassed an enormous army on the border that separated the two Kingdoms ready to take by force that which he wished to own.

The good King gathered his people together to form an army to defend their Kingdom and its river. But it was a small Kingdom, with a small untrained army compared to the size of the other with its warriors well-seasoned in the art of war.

Having crossed the border in the early morning while the grey mist lay low on the land the two opposing armies now faced each other on the green fertile fields below Moran Tor and the high dark mountains of Eslip.

The lark high on the wing watched as both armies sharpened their weapons in preparation for battle; then the tuneful bird started to mimic the song of the flute that was lodged far away in the reeds on the bank of the buttercup meadow; that same song, that same tune that helped make the river flow, the reeds grow through which the wind would gently blow.

The lark's song awakened new life in the discarded flute and with the help of the gentle wind it started to play of its own accord. And each reed on the river bank became a flute and took up the refrain sending it northwards, onwards to their river's source behind Moran Tor and the high dark mountains of Eslip where, in a bejewelled castle beside the sea of a mystical land deep in the earth lived a White Knight.

On hearing the tune high above as it swept across the land reverberating through the valleys and deep stone gulley's of the mountains, it fleetingly punctured and stirred a faint glimmer of recollection in an otherwise lost memory, then dulled and died as quickly as it had come. The White knight now tall in the saddle upon his white steed, galloping with great speed came up from where he dwelt at the source of the river and rode to the summit of Moran Tor.

Looking down he saw the two armies before him engaged in the fiercest of combat. The battle raged first this way then that way, backward and forwards across the field which once was green with succulent grass, now churned bare, and stained with pierced dead flesh and the blood of torn-limbed soldiers.

The White Knight lowered the visor on his helmet and with his mighty unsheathed sword raised high, he spurred on his white charger and galloped into the fray.

No sword, arrow, spear or lance could penetrate his white armour as he cut, thrust hacked and slaughtered the army of the wicked King. Those who managed to escape his fearful blows threw down their weapons, deserted their

King and in fear ran from the field as fast as their legs would carry them.

It was a quick, stroke from the White Knight's mighty sword that neatly removed the head from the body of the evil King; and there it lay in the slimy mud, its sightless eyes, a juicy breakfast for the carrion crow.

With the Kingdom and its river saved the White Knight was invited to attend the palace of the King so he could be formally thanked while partaking of food from a more lavish and pleasing choice of menu.

As he rode on his white horse towards the Royal residence, crowds lined the street cheering and joyfully waving flags. There was thanksgiving and merriment everywhere not only to celebrate a great victory, but this day of all days was their King's Birthday.

On one street corner there was a young man playing a flute surrounded by people dancing. Intrigued the White Knight reigned in his horse to a halt and for a moment watched, wondering what future might be in store for such a talented young man… then rode on.

At the palace the King waited on the regal stairway to greet the white armoured knight who had saved the Kingdom. Following a great fanfare and the official welcome the King led his guest into the lushly decorated throne room that had in its middle a pool of clear water fed by an ornate fountain. Here he quietly apologised for the absence of his daughter but as he did so, a little out of breath the Princess arrived. "Sorry I'm late father" she said, "I just felt that today I had to go down to the buttercup meadow beside the river."

"But you haven't been down there for years" said the King. "Why today of all days? Look, here we have a guest, a hero who has fought single-handed and saved our kingdom." The Princess turned and smiled at the White Knight. Her eyes were dark, like the deepest of secret pools, and her hair raven black, cascaded down to her slim waist. “Thank you” she said as she curtsied before him. “You are so very brave. I heard of your heroic deeds from a little bird high on the wing and for some reason I felt compelled to go down to the river.”

Never had the White Knight seen anyone so beautiful as the Princess and he fell in love with her there and then.

“One day daughter” said the king laughing “the river will swallow you, now off you go and get changed, while I talk to this brave young man.”

On leaving the room she suddenly stopped and glancing back over her shoulder she saw the early morning, light reflecting from off the clear water of the throne room pool creating a shimmering ripple effect across the face of the young knight. For one fleeting moment time seemed to stand still as a muddled thought struggled for clarity but then, that such thought vanished as quickly as it had come, and the Princess continued on her way.

“Now”, said the King “I and the people of this Kingdom are in your debt and most happy to be so, therefore what would you have? I can give you jewels, castles, lands and ships. You can have whatever you wish, they can all be yours, you only have to say”

“That is very kind of you” said the White Knight “but I have no need of jewels, castles, lands and ships for I have all those things but there is one thing I crave more than anything and that is the true love of a wife. Your majesty I find myself to be deeply in love with your daughter. May I ask her for her hand in marriage”?

“Indeed you may” said the King with great excitement. “What more could a father wish for his daughter, than she be married to such a brave knight. You have not only saved the Kingdom but wish to marry my daughter. This is indeed a joyful birthday. I will go at once and send her to you"

The King literally danced with joy across the throne room on his way to summon the Princess and as he left, with an almighty leap he kicked his heels and banged his head on the gold gilded door frame. Rubbing his wound and chuckling to himself he skipped off down a long marble corridor singing "Happy Birthday to me, Happy Birthday to me" until he eventually disappeared through an opening at the far end.

Not long after the Princess returned to the throne room. "Hello again" she said as she sat down beside the pool. The white knight standing there in his pristine white armour watched her with adoration. She looked at him and smiled.

"You are so beautiful with your dark eyes like the deepest of secret pools and your raven black hair cascading down to your slim waist." said the White Knight "and although I have only just met you, I love you with all my heart. I am rich and have a castle and land by the ocean where floats my fleet of fine ships. I own gold, silver and precious jewels that sparkle in the early morning sun. All will be yours if you will consent to marry me and be my loving wife"

Pensively the Princess studied the White Knight's reflection in the water of the ornamental pool and again for one fleeting moment time seemed to stand still and the shimmering image became that of the boy, the boy with the flute that she knew so long ago. And then the vision dissolved amidst a salty tear.

Wiping the wetness from her cheek she looked up and her gaze went far beyond the White Knight to where through the window she saw and heard the song of a Lark high on the wing.

"I thank you" said the Princess "I would be honoured to marry such a handsome brave Knight who saved the Kingdom but, I'm sorry I could never truly love you. For you see when I was a young girl, each day in the early morning I used to go down to the river and there was a young boy on the other bank who played the flute. His tunes were so beautiful they helped make the river flow, the reeds to grow through which the wind would gently blow. I fell in love with that boy and I knew then I could never truly love anyone but him. There by the river I made a promise to myself that whatever the future held for me I would never ever marry anyone else. One day I was taken ill, nothing serious just a bad cold, but my father insisted that I should stay in bed for a few days. The next time I was able to cross the buttercup meadow and go down to the water's edge the boy with the flute was not there. I went back day after day but still he did not return. Some people said the river had swallowed him. I felt such grief and emptiness at not seeing him sitting there leaning against a willow and playing his tunes; such beautiful tunes that helped make the river flow, the reeds to grow through which the wind would gently blow, that since then I never went back to the river… until today." "Not until today?" questioned the White Knight.

"No, but this very morning" the princess continued "I thought I felt him to be so near to me I went down to the river in the belief he would be sitting there on the other bank playing his flute with only the river to divide us, but it wasn't to be; he was not there. The only music and song came from a lark high on the wing."

"I quite understand" said the White Knight as he slowly walked away from the princess into the palace yard. A promise is a promise and as such must be kept but oh how I wish I could have been that boy for I would have waited for you until all the worlds rivers had run dry."

Then, mounting his white horse he blew her a gentle kiss and rode away following the river northwards, to its source behind Moran Tor and the high dark mountains of Eslip where he disappeared, never to be seen again… Some say the river swallowed him.

The river is flowing, flowing, flowing
The wind is blowing gently through the reed.

I first heard the basis of a similar story told by my good friend Sharon Aviv while we were performing a mini concert tour of Israel in 1999. I hope my version, my retelling does it justice.

The Mermaid of Upper Sheringham

or

A Twist to a Tale

Many years ago, off the windswept coast of Norfolk there lived a mermaid. As mermaids go, she wasn't that pretty nor was she ugly. Just a plain looking mermaid. However, like all the rest of her kind she had a voice so beautiful that when hungry she could lure many a seafarer to a watery grave. And there below the waves, so they didn't rise back to the surface when bloated, she would gather rocks and weight down their drowned pale wrinkled puckered corpses on the sandy seabed ready to feast on them one by one when the fancy took her.

Yet she wasn't selfish she let the lobsters, crabs and other such creatures gorge on the dead flesh at the many dinner party's she threw below the salty waves.

Maybe you the reader or you the listener find those actions somewhat, if not all together, distasteful (if you will please excuse the pun), but the Mermaid thought nothing of it. After all Jack Tar and landlubbers alike ate a fine harvest taken from the seas with nets, pots, line or harpoon. This mermaid had swum in all seven seas and had heard the anguished cry of a harpooned whale and seen the sea and shoreline awash with its blood. She had seen her friends the fishes in their thousands dropping like rain from nets on the wet slippery decks of boats and watched them being filleted alive.

So, to her, being in every sense of the word a daughter of the sea, it was quite natural to eat and enjoy human flesh. This mermaid wasn't some little, salt wouldn't melt in her moth, mermaid dreamt up by a Danish fantasist born in a fairy-tale-like cottage in Odense.

No, this Mermaid was tough, rough, mean, and a little overweight. She would never have fallen in love with a prince anyway but was not averse to dining on rich food if the opportunity presented itself.

One night, having found she was clean out of putrid bodies in the seabed larder, due to the fishes and crustaceans having been a little too greedy, and feeling a touch hungry herself she swam to the surface where she bopped about in the foamy waves some way out from the shore of the windmill-dotted Norfolk coastline. There she looked first towards the land for a lonely sailor on the beach who she could regale with her bewitching melodies, then towards the horizon.

Snow had started to fall, and vision became poor as the icy flakes became dense but at last, she spied a vessel, a full rigged Carrack, far out on the ocean heading for Yarmouth.

The mermaid started to sing to lure its crew to turn the vessel towards her that it might run aground on the chalk reef. Her sweet clear voice floated out over the waves and all those on hearing it, as it rode the north wind, fell into a trance.

The ship she could now see had altered its course. nearer and nearer it came towards the shallow waters of the reef where it would founder, become beached, crack its timbers and break its back tossing many sailors to their death in the icy cold sea.

Nearer and nearer it came towards the mermaid but then her seductive singing was eclipsed by another sound; the sound of bells as they joyfully rang out through the cold night air calling mortal folk to worship.

Sweet bells sweet chiming Christmas Bells
Sweet bells sweet chiming Christmas Bells
They cheer us on our Heavenly way
Sweet chiming Christmas Bells.

On hearing them the Captain awoke from the mermaids bewitching melodious trance and realising his ship was getting too near the charted reef, too near the shore, frantically he shouted orders to lower the foresheet, turn to port, show the land the ship's stern and tack towards deep water.

The mermaid furiously beat the waves with her tail while screaming in rage and cursing the bells that had deprived her of a decent meal. When her initial anger had subsided, she took time to listen. She had heard those bells many times before but this particular night there was a strangeness about their song, a strangeness that seemed to be drawing her in towards the shore, towards the Hythe where fishermen launched their boats to catch her friends.

Sweet bells sweet chiming Christmas Bells
Sweet bells sweet chiming Christmas Bells

"Appy Christmas" she heard someone shout. "Yis an' a roight 'appy Christmas to yew an'all, I'm oft tuh that there church for Mass. Will yew cum" came a reply from out of the darkness. "Noo' not me I's lollopen tuh the ale house to havva drink. I'll be fare drunk as a lord afore clock strikes twelve" was the response.

Ah', thought the Mermaid it is Christmas eve. She had heard sailors talk of such a night as they drunk rum and sung songs around an evergreen decorated mast to celebrate the birth of a baby boy then by all accounts ate him and drank his blood.

Naturally she herself didn't celebrate this night because she was a demonic creature of the aquatic world; but being by this time extremely hungry the thought of a meal of fresh human flesh washed down with blood was very appealing.

As the sound of human voices receded, she slithered her way across the shingle then keeping to the shadows she followed the call of the bells, up the hill to the ancient church. Just as they ceased their peel, she made her way through the latch gate into the churchyard. Exhausted by the long climb she stopped to take breath; then noticing the north door of the church to be slightly ajar, unseen she slid in.

She was immediately enthralled by the sheer beauty of the interior with its numerous candles radiating a soft warm shimmering light upon the cold stout lime mortar fixed flint walls. The church was full to bursting with people old and young comfortable in each other's company.

Out of sight of prying eyes she huddled in a dark corner and became spellbound by the lone pure voice of a young boy singing praises in honour of a new born babe. She had never heard a sweeter sound. It was a sound that took away the pains of hunger, as gently she was lulled asleep with a strange calm warm feeling of goodness somewhere deep in her chest between her naked breasts.

When she awoke, she found the church to be empty and in darkness except for one solitary candle; the parish Advent candle, illuminating a statue of a man holding an anchor. The sight of the anchor aroused her senses and she started to panic with the realisation she had over stayed her time on dry land, and she must quickly return to her home beneath the waves or she would die.

She frantically wriggled her tail sending herself skimming and skidding across the tiled floor back to the north door.

As much as she tried, the door would not open. Following the service, it had been securely locked by the Sexton. Even the font, had she known it contained water with which she could have dampened and re-energized her body and the scales of her tail, was locked to stop people stealing its blessed holy ingredient, as was the practice in those days.

Her strength was ebbing like the tide. She was becoming weaker by the minute. In desperation she looked up towards the statue for pity, for help. Its plaster eyes appeared to radiate a heavenly compassion as they looked back at her and in doing so drew her gaze down to a brass inscription near the floor which read 'St Clement Patron Saint of Mariners'.

Instantly she found herself earnestly begging for forgiveness, saying sorry for her wicked ways; apologising for causing the drowning and eating of so many seafarers. “Help me, help me” pleaded the Mermaid “I have been out of the water for too long. I am suffocating. I don't want to die.”

“No one wants to die; those sailors didn't want to die” rebuked the statue “but by the power of the Lord Jesus Christ their bless'ed souls are now in heaven.”

“But what of me” sobbed the Mermaid “I am a creature of the sea. I have no soul, where will I go, I can't go to heaven without a soul can I?”

“No” replied the statue “but here amongst living mortals you are only dead when no one remembers you, when no one says your name; when you are forgotten, erased from memory. That is when you will be truly dead and only then. One day”, he sighed “as sure as the tide flows in and flows out again I will be moved from here, where I stand, put away to gather dust in an old woodworm infested cupboard where, with time, I will crumble into a pile of clay powder to be swept away and forgotten. As the years pass by, eventually there will be no one who will remember that I had a prominent place here by this door and if in future years someone should mention the likes of me in a story, someone reading or hearing that story is sure to say there has never been a statue of St Clement in this church for as long as I can remember. But you Mermaid, you will remain here and will forever be alive in the minds of all who enter this place for here you will be, long after I have gone. You will be granted protection in this, Gods house, not because you have asked for forgiveness but because you will be looked upon, be wondered at and seen through the eyes of some as a work of art, by others an oddity, and by folk who have good imaginations – the reason for legend, the basis of a good story and by such means you will be immortalised."

"Now", said the statue softly "Drift as like wood upon an ocean's waves into the deepest sleep of all sleeps."

And there she is to this very day, asleep on the end of a pew by the north door of the village church of All Saints of Upper Sheringham in the county of Norfolk.

Touch her if you wish but remember... mermaids can bite.

Sweet bells sweet chiming Christmas Bells
Sweet bells sweet chiming Christmas Bells

Loosely based on an old but very short story I came across, on a plaque, in the church on my way back to the Holy Shrine of Our Lady of Walsingham following a very cold swim in the sea at Cromer, 5/10/2016.

The Rain Man

There were no ducks on the village pond. But why should there have been, there was no pond because it hadn't rained for weeks and weeks. Where the pond had once graced the idyllic English scene was now just a hollow of hard cracked earth. What reeds there were at its edge had long ago lost their greenness and were nothing more than short black withered stalks, but worst of all the annual village Fete and horticulture competition had yet again been cancelled. This in itself was a disaster especially for the Major whose cherished marrows now resembled nothing more than small shrivelled pickled gherkins.

"Damn bad show what" remarked the Major to the vicar of the ancient parish church of St Swithin. "What is" replied the respected man of the cloth as he tried not to be distracted from politely saying goodbye to each and every parishioner as they left the church following the Sunday morning service. "The weather damn it, Vicar, the weather. Hasn't rained for months what; months I say, bloody months. So, what are you going to do about it?" "What am I going to do about it" questioned the Reverend Hardpew.

"Yes, you" continued the Major raising his voice so that even frail old Miss Dorothy Quaver the organist (who's hearing was not good at the best of times) turned her head in alarm and played yet another wrong note. "You are in touch with Him aren't you" bellowed the Major "Who?" said the Reverend. "The Almighty that's who. Thought you chaps had a direct line to him, what old bean." "I don't think it's something I am able to achieve on my own" quietly countered the vicar who was anxious to remove his vestments and go home to his Sunday Lunch. "However, I will call a meeting of all the villagers and we can collectively work on this problem of the drought"

And that is exactly what happened; a week later, following evensong the local community assembled for the meeting presided over by the Reverend Hardpew in the village hall which was owned and attached to the church.

After the formalities of welcome naturally the Reverend Hardpew suggested that they prayed for rain and there was a small murmur of approval but then someone said "Well we do that every Sunday and it don't seemed to 'ave got us anywhere do it! I suggest we dance for rain" "Very well" said the vicar "Those who wish to pray for rain, pray for rain and those that wish to dance for rain, dance for rain." "Now 'ang on a bit vicar there's a few of us 'ere who fancy drumming for rain. What about us then!" enquired old Ned the village blacksmith who was quite accustomed to knocking out a regular and rhythmic beat with his hammer upon the anvil.

Then someone else shouted "It's all to do with being at one, communing with nature I want to hug a tree for rain" "Yes so do I" said another. "And I" agreed someone else who up till then had dozed off and had been snoring quite loudly having spent some time prior to the meeting popping out to the lavatory and smoking something that wasn't purely tobacco.

"Right then" said Harold for that was the vicar's Christian name, "Those who wish to pray for rain, pray for rain. Those of you who wish to dance for rain please dance for rain. Those who wish to drum for rain, then drum for rain and those who wish to hug trees for rain then do so."

With all that said the Reverend Harold Hardpew was just about to close the meeting when the door at the rear of the hall opened and there stood George, barely illuminated by the dim porch light.

George lived in a cottage, which many referred to as a hovel, outside the village just below the tree line at the bottom of Daisy Hill. Being happy in his own company he tended to keep himself to himself and there's nothing wrong with that.

"Can I help you George?" said Harold "I was just about to close the meeting. You are a little late." "No tis' alright Vicar I ain't come to no meeting" muttered George "Nite to yer" And with that George was gone.

Reverend Harold Hardpew scratched his head and closed the meeting by suggesting that if it failed to rain within the next two weeks, they should all meet again after evensong.

"I don't go to no bloody evensong" old Ned was heard to remark as he left the hall, merged with the outside darkness and disappeared into the night while Harold switched off the porch light, locked the outer door and himself headed for home.

Two weeks passed and still there was not a drop of rain, therefore the arranged meeting convened in the same manner embracing the same suggestions as before. There were those who wanted to continue to pray for rain, those that were still happy to dance for rain. Those who had found great joy in drumming for rain had no intention whatsoever in stopping and those who at first were into hugging trees for rain were now spending their time hugging each other and by the smiles of contentment on their faces they also had no intention of stopping even if did rain.

Just as that second meeting was coming to an end once again the door at the back of the hall opened and there again stood George who, due to faulty wiring, could only be seen intermittently lit by the dim porch light.

"Good evening George, you are most welcome, come on in" said Reverend Hardpew from where he was contacting the meeting on the dusty stage. "Ain't got the time" replied George as he turned on his heels and disappeared back out into shadows.

That meeting closed but not before another meeting was arranged in case it didn't rain within the following two weeks… which it didn't and the groups that were now gathered a fortnight later in the tiny church hall looked in a sorry state.

Those that had prayed for rain were complaining of sore knees and could hardly walk. Those that danced for rain trod slowly and carefully due to sore feet and backs. Those who drummed for rain had their hands bandaged and spoke loudly due to hearing loss and those that had first hugged trees for rain and then each other had gone one step further; all had found themselves a partner within their group and lustily and without hesitation each couple had run off together and were never seen again.

The Reverend Harold Hardpew was just about to slowly, painfully, climb up on to the stage in order to address the meeting when from behind the red frayed, dusty stage curtain out stepped George.

"I can make it rain" he calmly said, without any hint of authority for that wasn't his way. "Pardon" said Harold

"I can make it rain" repeated George, which created much laughter and ridicule amongst those assembled. "How can you make it rain?" they shouted.

"You come to my home, that one you call a hovel tomorrow morning and I will make it rain" said George. "You can't make it rain and we are certainly not coming up to Daisy Hill" they shouted

"Oh' yes I can, and I am sure I will see you all at my place in the morning 'cause I understands human nature I do" responded George in a serene tone.

Sure enough, just like George had predicted, the following day as the sun began to raise over Daisy Hill up and down the village street doors slowly opened and silently the occupants of many a thatched cottage stepped out into the early morning light and made their way towards the hill and George's home. Ned the blacksmith with hands bandaged wisely decided not to attempt to fire up the furnace and quietly attached himself to the back of the hushed procession as did Reverend Harold Hardpew who had decided to forego morning prayer and had been assessing his faith under the canopy of the wilting churchyard yew tree.

As the inquisitive file of people reached the Georgian Manor House the Major, without hesitation and taking a swig of a tot or two of brandy from an engraved silver hip flask, immediately placed himself at the front of the column muttering "Good turnout, damn fine show what."

At last the early morning walkers reached their destination and there standing behind two trestle tables was George looking very fresh and sprightly for that time of day. "So, you all decided to come after all. I knew you would because I understand human nature" he said as he greeted each of his guest with a nod of his head and a wry smile.

"Get on with it" shouted the blacksmith "make it rain" "Yes come on, you said you could make it rain" shouted the others as they moved menacingly towards George. "And I will" said George "but first would someone please fetch me a bowl of water" "And where would we get a bowl of water it hasn't rained for months" the crowd shouted. furiously. "Oh someone will have a bowl of water 'cause I understands human nature I do" said George calmly.

It would be wrong of me, the writer of this tale, to point a finger and expose the person who eventually returned with a bowl of water except to say that a number of baptisms were still taking place over the period of the drought.

As soon as the bowl was placed in front of him George removed his shirt and there and then in front of the now speechless villagers, he proceeded to wash that particular article of clothing in a most carefree manner with a bar of cracked soap which up till then had been concealed in his trouser pocket.

"Could someone fetch me another bowl of water please" inquired George having produced a scrubbing brush from another pocket with which he feverishly attacked the collar and cuffs.

"Now look here old chap" said the Major "this is a damn poor show; what! Water, there is no water that's why we are here what! No water in the desert either what! Now I remember when my troops and I…" "Someone will have a bowl of water" interrupted George "'course I understands human nature I do." And indeed he did.

Again, it's not my place as the writer and teller of this tale to point a finger but Ned the Blacksmith still tempered and quenched metal in his forge and not long after George had called for another bowl of water another bowl, although looking a little sooty, was placed next to the first one.

Amid cries of anger and despair George casually removed his shirt from the first bowl and rinsed it out in the second. The crowd surged forward but before they could physical harm George, for that was their intention George stepped to one side and hung his shirt on a tree to dry. It was then and only than that dark rain clouds rapidly formed over Daisy Hill and a tremendous clap of thunder announced the return of a traditional British summer of cold wet rain.

Amongst the jubilation, praise and thanks were showered on George. But one important question was on the minds of the villagers standing there happily drenched.

"Damned good show what!" spluttered the Major. "Praise the Lord" sung the vicar. "There's a hole in the church roof" gasped the organist Miss Quaver, who was always late getting up and had only just arrived. "And mine" complained the Blacksmith; "the rain is sure to dampen the coals and stop me lighting the bloody furnace when me 'ands are better."

"Well come on man tell us how you did it bawled the Major How did you make it rain, what!" "It always rains when I wash my shirt" said George. "What", exploded the Major "Then why, you damn buffoon didn't you wash it months ago?" "It wasn't dirty" then said George as he went into his cottage some called a hovel.

Based on a speck of a story I remember hearing at a Sidmouth Folk Festival.

Fionn MacCumhaill/Finn McColl

Between the deep blue sky and the silvery sea in the land that poets call the Emerald Isle there lived a giant of a man, a great hero warrior who had never been defeated in battle or in love. So many tales of his heroic deeds abound but for you my reader I have chosen but just this one which I believe has a message for us all.

One evening after a hard day's battle against Rican, a troublesome mountain troll, Finn McColl, feeling uncommonly tired, yawned and sprawled himself out on the top of a huge granite boulder under which our hero's grotesque adversary now lay decidedly dead and compressed thinner than a wafer on a knickerbocker glory.

As twilight shadows began to reach out across the lush green grasses of the fertile land, with Bran his faithful sharp fanged hunting dog snuggled by his side, Finn McColl fell into a deep sleep and in doing so quietly slipped across the wispy threshold into the land of vibrant dreams; a land where legends are born, and stories unfold.

Bran suddenly pricked up his ears, sniffed the air than ran off at full speed towards the deep mysterious forests of the Slieve Bloom Mountains.

"Where you be' going? Come back here It's getting dark, time we went home" shouted Finn McColl but Bran had a mindset of his own and kept running and eventually disappeared into the bushes below the dense leafy canopy of the dark wood.

Finn McColl eventually tiring of calling Bran to heel, retrieved his sword from where he had left it prior to using the boulder as his weapon of choice to slay the irritating troll and made his way down the grassy slope following in the tracks of his wilful hound.

When Finn McColl reached the forest, he searched deep amongst the trees but of Bran there was no sign; only gossamer winged fairy folk darting hither and thither like fireflies while in a high-pitched language (you dear reader would not understand unless, of course like me, you believe in fairies) they welcomed Finn and thanked him for ridding their world of such a distasteful repugnant troll. Then those same tiny folk gathered together into one bright ball of shimmering light and without further ado, flying very close past Finn's ear, they left the forest, which had until then been their refuge, and returned to their fairy ring kingdoms deep beneath the rich Irish soil.

No sooner had they gone than a strange mist brought a chill to the air as it descended from the mountains and tumbled, swirled and twirled its way through the trees. Finn wrapped his cloak around him for warmth and calling out again for Bran he waited expectantly for him to come bounding towards him crashing noisily through the dense undergrowth while vigorously wagging his tail in canine celebration of a rabbit or a squirrel clasped firmly between his jaws. But it wasn't to be; of his dog there was still no sign.

Apart from the sound of Finn McColl's own breathing all was silent. Not a leaf could be heard to rustle in the darkness of that wood. Some say even the mice wore carpet slippers.

Firmly grasping his sword, he ventured further and further amongst the leaves until suddenly the mist lifted and he found himself in a glade where stood a turf roofed stone cottage with its door wide open and from the chimney, smoke twirled effortlessly high into what was now a star buttoned sky.

Finn strode up to the welcoming door and knocked three times with the hilt of his blade on the age worn weathered timber frame. From inside there came no sound other than the crackling of wood upon the open fire. “That's strange” he thought and knocked again a little harder but still there was no sound other than that of the fire. He peered into the room and saw sat by the blazing hearth a beautiful young woman with dark eyes and long jet-black hair. Such was her beauty it instantly took his breath away. Throughout his life he had seen and been with many young beautiful looking women but never had he seen any nearly so adorable as she who sat there in silence gazing attentively into the eyes of a very old man sitting opposite whose white beard flowed down over to his knees and across the stone floor to where stood a goat at the door.

“Might I come in? I'm looking for my hound and I'm feeling a touch cold and a wee bit tired” said Finn McColl. “If you want to” said the woman, not for one second averting her eyes away from those of the old man. Finn stepped over the goat, walked the carpet of white hair and sat down beside the woman. Sitting so close he could smell the fragrance and the tantalizing freshness of her body. As his heart took on a faster rhythm, he felt an overwhelming need to touch, kiss and caress the beautiful soft pale skin of the youthful woman; taste the wetness of her lips and gently stroke her long jet-black hair. Moving closer he whispered in her ear and no sooner had he done so she stood up, took him by the hand and led him into a small room at the back of the tiny cottage. The door closed behind them.

The sounds of passion emerging from that room I feel it best I leave to you my reader to conjure from your own imagination. However, following a long spell of activity eventually there was silence; a long silence. Then the door opened and out came the woman and sat down again facing the old man; followed, a few moments later, by a somewhat dishevelled Finn McColl wearing a broad smile, who again sat next to the woman and after some considerable time when he had regained his strength said "You are so beautiful and were so wonderful to me I want you again." "If you want me again" said the woman "then first you must fight and overcome this old man who sits opposite."

"That man?" said Finn "But I am Finn McColl, a warrior, and a great hero of all Ireland. If that frail, wrinkle-skinned, old man was just to stand, his bones would instantly creak and snap, putting him down on the hard-earthen floor before I would have had the chance to take a breath and blow him over. But if to overcome that white-bearded old man is all I need to do to have you again" said Finn "then so it shall be." And so saying he reached for his sword and as he did so, the fail wrinkle-skinned old man without even bothering to get up from where he was sitting in one move disarmed and brought down the great hero Finn McColl with a loud thud to the ground from where now the great warrior found himself looking up and along his own razor sharp blade that was being held against his throat. The old man looking down at him paused for a moment then without a word, slightly just very slightly nicked the skin, with the tip of the blade, just below Finns Adams Apple, then gave the sword back to Finn and without a word resumed staring into the eyes of the woman.

Finn McColl was not only totally defeated but also utterly confused as to how he, the champion of the Fenian and hero of all Ireland, could have been beaten by an old white-haired man. Embarrassed, he slowly got up and turning to the woman said "I am so sorry, this has never happened to me before. I must have tripped on the old man's beard. Is there anything else I could do instead? "Yes, there is" she said. "That goat by the door; the one you stepped over when you came in, please move it out of the way."

"Certainly" said Finn. "That will be no problem at all." And with that he went over to the door and started to push and shove the goat, but it wouldn't budge and even pulling on its horns in an attempt to drag it away from the door he failed miserably. Only one thing for it thought Finn McColl and that was to lift it like he had the huge granite boulder with which he had triumphantly squashed the troll. He then stood back, eyed up the scraggy goat, put his arms, head and shoulders under the belly of the animal and attempted to lift the stubborn creature but it didn't matter how much he tried it stayed firmly rooted to the spot. Not a fraction of an inch did Finn raise it from the floor. Exhausted and wiping the beads of sweat from his brow Finn McColl fell to his knees and turning to the woman said, "Who are you and what is this strange place?" "The goat" she replied "is death. No matter how much you try to push it away it will always stand there at the door. The old man represents old age however much you try to defeat it, it will always overcome you. And me, I am youth. I was yours once and I will never be yours again."

Before the last rays of the sun had completely disappeared to leave the remaining daytime shadows to join those of the night Finn McColl, who was still laying sprawled out fast asleep on the huge granite boulder, was suddenly but affectionately woken from his dream by a cold wet nose and slobbering tongue on his face.

Sitting up, he immediately hugged Bran his faithful hunting dog then slid down the rock to the ground. "Sorry" he said "I must have dozed off. I expect you want your dinner." Bran wagged his tail. Picking up his sword Finn McColl noticed, at the very tip of the blade, there was the tiniest speck of what looked like blood. As he wiped away the stain on the sleeve of his emerald green jacket a chillness penetrated his very core enticing him to feel his neck and on doing so, he shivered with the sudden realisation that even great heroes don't live forever.

Based on an Irish story I first heard told by my good friend and fellow storyteller Sharon Aviv whilst we toured Israel in 1999 telling stories at various venues.

The Devil and the Fiddler

Once a week on a Thursday evening a small group of devoted musicians, singers and storytellers met in the low beamed tap room of the Fiddlers Arms. Each and every one of them dedicated to keeping the old folk traditions alive as well as the local brewery. Yes, devoted campaigners for real ale they were with their seemingly never-ending endeavours to drink their landlord dry which on the face of it when all was said and done was nigh impossible to do bearing in mind Allen the landlord owned the little brewery in a slated roof outhouse behind the pub.

Good news all-round one would think; however, times were getting hard partly due to the new road bypassing this old-world establishment plus rising overheads for such things as malt and barley. Customers had become fewer and fewer so naturally takings were down and although the talented Thursday evening folk crowd brought the place alive, sadly for the rest of the week hardly a soul graced this picturesque grade two listed building in its quiet winding lane beside the clear cool meandering river. It was coming to a point when the landlord was seriously considering selling to one of the big commercial breweries. No sooner had he made some loose inquiries in that direction the pressure was on and he had become inundated with letters and visits from men in sleek suits and loud ties brandishing reams of official papers in their chubby, floppy workshy hands.

To give him his due, at first, he shunned them all and remained loyal to what few customers he did have, especially the Thursday evening Folkies with their personalised pewter tankards who likewise stayed loyal to him and his liberal attitude to drinking after hours, which was certainly a bonus.

It was the strangest of circumstances that changed everything, and it all started on one Thursday evening in October.

The group had met, and Joe had started off the evening with a rendering of the Scottish ballad Tamlin which resulted in, from those still awake, a tremendous applause for remembering all forty-two verses; if for nothing else.

Malcolm was next to contribute to the evening playing various dance tunes on his melodeon and so it was between bouts of chatting the evening progressed. Harps, dulcimers whistles and bodhrans all featured that evening some being played with great sensitivity and some with manic gusto. Just before the break when the landlord produced, as he always did, a selection of savoury sandwiches as a goodwill gesture for the entertainers a stranger entered the bar. He carried a fiddle case and politely asked if he could play. "Indeed you can" said Kiti, a fine singer who had assumed the position of as Master of Ceremonies for the evening "We will be starting again in a minute or two you can follow Deborah, who is going to give us a couple of tunes on the concertina."

With all the food now consumed and the group having replenished their tankards the second half of the evening commenced with Deborah playing with perfection a couple of well-rehearsed Irish reels followed by a long discussion about the source of the tunes and the various keys they could be played in.

At last the floor was given over to the newcomer who introduced himself as Mark while he unhurriedly opened the case, took out the fiddle gave it a leisurely clean with a yellow duster then slowly tightened the strings of the bow. As he meticulously placed the fiddle under his chin the room fell silent so much so you could have heard a pin drop on the scrubbed wooden floor. All those present held their breath in anticipation as Mark placed the tensioned bow on the first string in E.

Slowly he moved the bow backwards and forwards scratching and scraping across the thin steel string. Then with a tilting of his wrist he proceeded to attack the other strings in the same fashion. Quite oblivious to the expressions of utter disbelief on the faces of all the accomplished musicians and other persons, who by now had the misfortune of being there in the bar having their hearing assaulted, he continued to scratch and scrape, for a full three minutes, what he believed to be a pleasant tune.

The applause was understandably somewhat subdued but Kiti politely thanked Mark for his contribution and turning towards the audience with eyes raised and a nonchalant smile made the mistake by saying “Hope to see you again.” which brought a broad smile to Mark's face as he resumed his seat. At eleven the landlord bolted the door and the second half of the evening continued until just before twelve when the last song was sung. Outside wrapped up warm against a biting autumn chill, farewells and good wishes were exchanged before all parted company.

The following week Kiti who once again was organising the evening quickly regretted her previous week's mistake when, just before the second part of the evening was about to start, into the room came Mark requesting to play. “I realise” he said “I wasn't that good last week I was somewhat nervous in front of a new crowd. “A new crowd?” replied Kiti. “Oh' yes” he said I have played at many clubs and gatherings like yours, but I have found the people to be most rude towards me and my playing. So much so I have not returned. But here you were all so very polite and applauded my music. You yourself said hope to see you again. Therefore, here I am happy to return, and I have spent the whole week practising some new tunes." "Em, ah' that's nice" said Kiti stammering to find the right words of enthusiasm. "Would you like to go on now?" she found herself saying as brightly as she possibly could under the circumstances. "Yes if you don't mind, I have a couple of tunes for you this evening" Mark replied while removing his fiddle from its case. "Just one would be lovely, always leave them wanting more" lied Kiti. And that said, with fingers crossed behind her back she introduced Mark for the second week running.

For you my reader I will not beat about the bush; Mark was no better at playing the fiddle that second week than he had been the first but politeness in that tap room prevailed then as it did up until the evening of the sixth week when the patience of one long suffering member of the audience ran out and he decided to put all courtesy aside and vent his feelings by telling Mark just what he thought of his playing and even suggested where he could put his fiddle and the bow. Others there, emboldened by the solitary outburst, now joined in with expressing their own unfavourable opinions regarding the screeching and scratching sounds produced from such a beautiful instrument.

Mark was momentary stunned by this outburst then he quickly picked up his fiddle, bow and case and stormed out of the pub shouting "The devil take you all."

It was on his way home that he stopped at the bridge where, looking over the side, he studied the reflection of the full moon in the clear water below. As he contemplated throwing the fiddle case and its contents into the flowing river he suddenly saw as part of the moons reflection a man standing behind him wearing a sleek suit and a loud tie, carrying some official looking papers. "No need to turn around" said the man. "Just keep looking at the reflection and tell me what it is that's bothering you that makes you consider throwing away your fiddle." Startled by the question but not looking back Mark enquired as to how the man knew what he was considering doing. Laughing the stranger said "Let's just say I make it my business. I know" he continued "that if you were to think about your playing then deep down in your soul you would except what others have told you in all the clubs and pubs you have embarrassingly performed. The fact is you can't play that fiddle of yours. I myself have heard you scratching and scraping across its poor strings. I have always been there in the shadows listening to the people laughing at you behind your back. He can't play that thing and never will be able to they say, and I agree with them one hundred percent. Mark you will never be able to play the fiddle because you are tone deaf. You haven't a chance in hell unless, of course you were to ask for my help."

"You rcally could help me?" said Mark not looking back and concentrating on the reflection off the water. "It is in my power to do so" said the stranger looking down and fingering his tie. "The next time you go to the Fiddlers Arms I could have you playing to a standard far beyond your wildest dreams. All you have to do is agree to my condition and sign my contract" "And what is your condition" asked Mark. "Quite simply this" said the other "you must never be playing at the first stroke of midnight because…" "No problem" said Mark interrupting the stranger in mid-sentence. So keen was he that everyone should admire his playing he grabbed the pen being offered and signed the document there and then under the full moon. "So be it" said the man in the sleek suit and loud tie. Then displaying a sinister grin, he took up the contract and turning around he slowly dissolved into his own watery reflection.

Mark didn't see the stranger's red barbed tail for he had been too busy looking at his watch to see if there was time before twelve just to play a tune or two. And there was for it was only a quarter to ten. So, putting the fiddle under his chin he slowly engaged the bow. Mark himself was utterly amazed at the quality of sound he was then producing as his bow tenderly embraced one after another the four strings without one screech scrape or scratch. It was as if a door, which until then had been firmly closed had opened to enhance his hearing and with such he had become as one with the instrument he was playing. He briefly tried one tune after another jigs, reels, waltzes whatever the tune whatever the tempo they all faultlessly danced off the strings and graced the air by the river that chill evening in the season of falling leaves.

A week passed and Mark with dogged determination decided to revisit The Fiddlers Arms and show off his newly acquired talent. Boldly walking through the door into the tap room he was greeted with objectionable mutterings from those folkies already assembled. As he went up to Kiti she smiled, nodded her head, stepped to one side and quickly said "I'm not MC this evening. Its Steve over there." 'Steve over there' turned out to be the chap who the previous week led the impolite protest against Marks playing and having spotted him and overheard what Kiti had just said he hastily addressed Mark with "Sorry mate, all slots are taken. No time this evening for any more performers." Undaunted Mark unhurriedly opened the case, took out the fiddle gave it a leisurely clean with a yellow duster. "I said all slots are taken. We are here to keep tradition alive, not kill it. Now be off with you" said Steve in his authoritarian MC voice. Mark slowly tightened the strings of the bow. "I said be off with you" repeated Steve irritably.

As Mark meticulously placed the fiddle under his chin the room, led by Steve, broke into an uproar of impolite words and gestures so much so that Allen the landlord was in fear of his establishment being torn apart.

Oblivious to the melee surrounding him Mark unhurriedly fine-tuned the hand-crafted instrument then came again as one with his fiddle while the clear perfect notes of his playing graced their way through the room which rapidly fell silent in dumbfounded awe at what was being heard. When Mark had completed a set of Morris Dance tunes the room of hecklers now sat with mouths agape. All were so completely transfixed that even if a box of nails had been dropped it would not have cut through the silence. Then, the audience in one accord snapped out of their trance like state, rose to their feet and gave a standing ovation begging for more. Mark was only too happy to oblige and played jigs, reels and all besides. Not once did anyone enquire about the fantastic transformation in Mark's ability at playing the fiddle for to do so would have meant a break in the wonderful music which had softened their antagonistic stance.

The evening continued with just Mark entertaining with tune after tune that even he himself was amazed at how many he seemed to know and was able to play. The only time he paused was to re-rosin his bow or to drink the pints of pub brewed ale bought for him in appreciation of his wonderful playing.

To the sound of great cheering at eleven thirty the landlord bolted the door and drew the curtains to signify a 'Lock-In' while Mark happily played on. Never in his life had so much attention been shown towards him and never had he drunk so much. At ten minutes to twelve, through blood shot eyes, he glanced up at the clock and remembered something about not playing on the first stroke of midnight because... “Because what?” he found himself saying out load. “What's that?” said Steve. “I think I had better stop now It's getting late.” replied Mark “Come on we have a 'lock in', nothing to worry about” slurred the evenings M.C as he tried to retain his balance. “You are great. Thank you for keeping the folk tradition alive, such wonderful playing. A few more tunes to round off the evening if you would.” “Very well” said Mark I have a few more minutes so one more tune and that's it. Any requests?” “What about The Devil's Dream” called out a man who was standing in the shadows at the back of the room. “Yes, then The Devil's Dream it shall be I have time for that” said Mark and he started to play. But you my reader and I both know that time can seem to fly by when we don't won't it too and so it was in this particular case. With his eye on the clock faster and faster he played as he watched the minutes pass by. The crowd were in raptures having never heard the Devil's Dream played so fast and with such skill and were instantly on their feet and with limbs akimbo frenziedly dancing.

At two minutes to twelve Mark decided to bring the tune to an abrupt halt but found he couldn't. The fiddle stayed as if glued to his chin. His fingers wouldn't stop fingering the strings as his bow arm involuntarily allowed hair to meet string. Panic set in as he tried to free himself, to stop himself playing. Then as the clock struck the midnight hour there was a tremendous flash of light and the sound of hideous demonic laughter from the man who stepping out of the shadows was seen to be wearing a sleek suit and loud tie as he disappeared down through the scrubbed wooden floor boards. Of Mark there was no sign; he had completely vanished and where he had stood playing now in his place was an old but fully functional sixties juke box. The Devil's music has been played in that establishment ever since and in doing so has attracted a younger crowd; the majority of whom have no appreciation of folk music or of keeping the old traditions alive.

Sadly, Allen the landlord succumbed and accepted an offer he couldn't refuse, from a man wearing a sleek suit and loud tie who worked for one of the big commercial breweries. Then as so often happens when a big named brewery become the new owners of a pub, they feel obliged not only to change its character but also its name. In this case from The Fiddlers Arms to...... The Devil's Fiddler.

I myself still occasionally go there on a Thursday evening and tell, if asked, this story for a few pints between bouts of loud head banging music with its inaudible lyrics but I don't have to cross any bridge to get there and back and what's more I would never ever tell this story or any other near midnight because, these days I like to be tucked up and in bed by eleven.

The root of this story was influenced from the telling of a similar story by Taffy Thomas MBE at Cecil Sharp House home of the English Folk Dance and Song Society.

Why

"Why" said the young camel to its father who was busy preparing to spit at something. Something he didn't particularly like. "Why do we have these wide strange looking feet with only two toes?"

"Well" said his father "The Creator gave us feet called hooves like this so that we would not sink in the desert sands and to give us a firm grip on rough ground. Will that be all because I'm quite busy at the moment"

"Oh" said the calf looking down at its hooves and mulling over in its mind what its father had just said before turning back to size up the intended target.

"Why Dad" continued the young camel "why do we have these strange humps on our backs?"

"Well", said his father, a little annoyed that its young offspring had again interrupted what he was doing. "Our humps store fat, not water as some humans tend to believe, although the fat can be converted to water and gives us energy when food is in short or no supply, which often it is in the desert... Now can I get on?" "Of course Dad" said the youngster, "but... well there is another thing" "Yes and what's that?" replied the father a little more than agitated because he had now worked out the exact distance between him and the target.

"It's these long eyelashes" said the young inquisitive camel. "Why have we got such long eye lashes?"

"Because" said the father. And although wishing to straightway follow through with his plan he was proud that his calf asked such questions, for to ask questions is a way to learn. "We have these long eye lashes so that when the desert winds blow and whip up a sand storm that sand won't get in our eyes."

"Thank you Dad" said the young studious camel. "I now understand why our hooves are like they are, so that they don't sink in the sands of a desert and to give us a firm grip on rough ground. I also realise now why we have a hump because it stores fat which can be converted to water and gives energy when food is in short supply or there is none at all which in the desert often is the case. Yes, and about the eyelashes I also understand, for as you told me it's to protect our eyes when the winds blow in the desert and whip up a sand storm."

"Good, well done" said the young camel's father as he moved a little to the left.

"Please tell me why then" replied the young scholarly camel... "why did the Creator think we would need such things here in a zoo?"

At that point the young camel's father, now with a tear in his eye, again viewed his target, viewed the angle, viewed the distance and then spat directly upon the face of the man who, regardless of the protests from his young grandchild, had continually poked the camel with his walking stick as it stood there, captive in its wire enclosure.

I first heard a snippet of this story in a noisy pub in west Hanningfield, Essex.

The Teller was Martin Murrell of Rayleigh Essex.

The New Recruit

Ever since the Christmas when he first received a tin drum and a box of lead soldiers it had always been his ambition, his goal, to become a soldier and serve his queen and country.

Guardsmen they were, those soldiers, wearing scarlet tunics and tall black Bearskins with bayonets fixed on rifles over their left shoulders in the slope arms position. When they had first arrived in their yellow box with its lid depicting Windsor Castle tiny hands with great precision paraded those rough cast troops in ranks of two where they didn't move an inch. Upright they were, fearless they stood wherever they were put. Yes, there was discipline in the ranks; not once did they disobey an order.

As the Christmases and birthdays rolled by, he accumulated more and more from Aunts, Uncles, and other friends of the family who were grateful they didn't have to wrack their brains to think what to get him and endlessly traipse around shop after shop looking for a present. They just bought him a box of soldiers. Of course, it wasn't long before they became plastic; the lead ones having become very expensive as collector's items. It also wasn't long before the young boy commanded a whole regiment of tiny warriors and if the aging process hadn't intervened, he would have possibly commanded a division or even a brigade.

He was now 18 and had worked hard at school and although he certainly wasn't the brightest academically, on the playing field he excelled. This was where he showed his real potential not only as a member of the football and cross-country teams in the winter months and the cricket team in the summer; but he was also a force to be reckoned with at track and field events. The gymnasium was also his domain. The box, the pommel, the beam, the floor or the trampoline, he could do them all equally as well with great agility, style, and panache.

But now it was time to fulfil his life's dream and off he marched to the local recruiting office.

“Yes son” said the somewhat formidable recruiting sergeant “and what can we do for the likes of you”? “I want to join up please” replied the seventeen-year-old. “So you want to serve do you, take the Queen's shilling, be a soldier, become a man in the army of 'er Majesty, God Bless 'er” “Yes Sir” stuttered the lad “I ain't no sir” the sergeant bawled and then speaking in a hushed voice said “that's for them posh people like 'im in there that is. Right in you go lad so's the Medical Officer can decide if you're fit enough.”

It was really only the matter of a quick cough for the Medical Officer, an aptitude test for an officer of the Royal Army Education Corp and in no time at all the young man was signing the papers of enlistment, in front of another Officer but this time a Lt. Colonel. “I take it you have fully read all the information in the brochure about life in the army?” enquired the officer as he sat there twiddling his moustache. “Oh yes” said the teenager having hastily read the information “it's going to be even much better than I thought and ever dreamt it would be.” “Well, I'm pleased to hear that” remarked the Commanding officer; for that's what the Lt Colonel was. “Sign here on the dotted line and accept your first week's pay, the Queen's shilling as it is known. You will receive your travel warrant to your training camp by post in the next few days. Don't forget to change at Crewe. Everyone changes trains at Crewe. “Good luck, I'm sure you will rise to great heights with us.”

“Thank you Sir I will do my very best” acknowledged the young man who wasn't sure if he should salute or not. The Colonel noticed the hesitation as he stood up then turned his back to gaze out of the window "Off you go then don't stand there dawdling. You are in the army now" he said over his shoulder as he watched a child happily playing with a box of toy soldiers on the waste ground just below the window ledge. Oh, to be that child again he thought to himself.

When the newly enlisted recruit arrived home and told his parents where he'd been and what he had done they were a little shocked by the news but not altogether surprised.

"So", said the lad's father "what convinced you that the Army would be the life for you?" "Well, replied his son "as you know, since I was given my first set of lead soldiers I have always wanted to join up and glancing through this brochure I just knew it would be right for me." "I'll just make a nice cup of tea while you two are chatting" said the boy's mother as she made her way out to the newly fitted kitchen.

"It's all in here" the young man continued "listed in this glossy broacher; free food, free clothing, free accommodation, and when I have finished 12 weeks basic training I will be posted to Germany. I can't wait to visit Hamburg and its Red Light District the Reeperbahn because it also says I will get free..." "Teacakes anyone?" interrupted his mother as she walked back in from the kitchen. "Free what?" questioned the father as he took the booklet to read. Then shaking his head, slowly from side to side, in realisation of his son's lack of literacy skills, exasperated he said "I do wish you'd learn to take your time and read things properly son. This doesn't say what you think it does. It says free parachutes."

"Oh my God" yelled the lad, his face turning an ashen grey, "I signed up for a hundred jumps."

Based on a short joke from my army days.

Toys Past

Dark dolls, fair dolls, with pretty china faces,
Model horses, rocking horses, hobby horses for our races.
Wax Crayons, Teddy bears, humming tops a-spinning,
Party masks painted sad, some gaily painted grinning.
Punch and Judy, Beelzebub and puppets hung on string,
Giants, trolls, Elfin knights and fairies in a ring.
Wooden forts and castles with soldiers made of lead,
Smartly paraded in a line with tunics of the brightest red.
Boats, trains, bats, balls and shiny perambulators,
Mechanical toys from Germany, such as clockwork alligators.
Wind-up mice, for girls not nice, but for boys, such great fun,
And little men who walk down slopes or can be made to run.
Readings for a lantern show with slides of Peter Pan
And a ball on string with a wooden cup,
for to catch it if you can.
Magic tricks, silly jokes, pop-up books so neat,
Skipping ropes and hoops of iron for playing in the street.
Grimaldi clowns that somersault, either fast or slow,
Harlequins and columbines ready for a show
In a model theatre also on display-
As cut-outs glued to rods of wood is how they act their play.
Telescope, microscope, kaleidoscope are there,
Shadowgraph, pantograph and a jig doll dancing bear,
And there is Jack upon a spring in a box of painted tin-
Release the catch upon the lid and you will never keep him in.

Diablos, whipping tops, houses for a doll
Five stones, Tarot cards, glass marbles for to roll,
Pairs of skates for frozen ponds, toboggans which go so fast,
Mittens and mufflers to wrap up warm
now winter's come at last.
Fine-tuned whistles they abound, as do big loud drums:
All small boys wish for one of those
when Father Christmas comes.

I wrote the poem Toys Past in 1987 as part of my play Long Gone Are the Days a section of which was broadcast on BBC Radio Essex at Christmas that same year.

Now You Have A Story to Tell

Name and age are of no importance to this tale, only that he was a young man who had been abandoned as a child and left to make his own way in the world, fend for himself and live by his wits. He could snare a rabbit, net a pheasant and tickle a trout. Well he knew the seasons; the freshness of Spring, the heat of Summer followed by Autumn's dampness proceeding the bitter cold iron fist of Winter. It was those times of the rolling year that mostly determined where he could find his next meal and where to lay his head for the night; be it beneath a hedgerow under a blanket of dusty discarded sacking or illicitly amongst the straw and odour of a cattle barn.

One day news was afoot that a hiring fair was to be set up in the market square. On impulse our young man decided he would attend, seek employment and better himself.

So, there he was in no time at all standing on a hastily constructed trestle stage alongside other men and woman seeking work, and this really is where my story begins.

Jobs on offer were various and as it was a rural town many were for craftsmen, Thatcher's, Blacksmiths, Carters and the like. For the woman work was to be had up at the Manor. Cook assistant, Lady's Maid, Scullery maid to name but a few positions on offer to the fairer sex. But of cause all such positions for both male and female were subject as to what was financially accepted in the bidding.

By late afternoon our youth was standing on his own. All the others who had put themselves up for hire that day had indeed been hired and were about their business with their new employer.

The young man was on the point of leaving the stage when a farmer approached him and said. “Youngman, I have been watching you with great interest. You stood there all day but didn't step forward for any of the jobs that were offered. Why was that?” “Cause” came the reply “I didn't know 'ow to do none of them jobs. I never 'ad no proper job before. I ain't trained like them that got them jobs and 'fore you asks I ain't never been to school and got an ed'umercation.”

“Well” said the farmer “I think myself to be somewhat benevolent and if you would like to come with me to my farm where I live with my wife I am willing to take you in as part of the family and teach you all the different jobs around a farm and not only that I will pay you fairly each week while you learn. How do you feel about that?”

Knowing winter was fast approaching and although wondering what the catch might be the young man somewhat hesitantly accepted the generous offer.

There was however nothing untoward in the proposal; the farmer was true to his word as true as there is salt in the sea. The youth settled in well and worked hard. The days turned into weeks, the weeks to months and the year turned around again.

It was a Sunday and the three of them, the youth, the farmer and his wife set off for church as was more the custom then than it is today. On their return home they sat down for a wonderful roast lunch of which to be fair to you the reader I won't go into any detail for fear you might drool and dribble upon the page before you. Needless to say it was a fine traditional Sunday Lunch after which, with bellies full and minds content, they all sat down for a quiet snooze by the hearth with the only sounds being that of the occasional spitting of logs on the grate of a blazing fire and the rattle of a loose window pane as the persistent cold wind tried in vain to enter this snug abode.

Then, all of a sudden, the farmer gets up, goes to the back room and brings out a case containing a fiddle and bow. He rosins the bow, places the fiddle under his chin and plays a merry tune to which his wife, holding her skirts, dances a fine jig.

When all was done, he puts the fiddle and bow back in its case and returns it from where it came as his jovial wife red cheeked and out of breath sits back in her chair.

The farmer then turns to the young man and says, "your turn" "What" protested the youth I can't play the fiddle. "No, no" replied the farmer "We don't expect you to but what about a story, we love a good story." "Don't know no story" insists the irritated youth and all three stared at the fire and watched the flames do their own dance making irregular shadow patterns on walls and ceiling until at last it was time for bed.

A week passed and all happened just the same as before; church, lunch, snooze, tune and dance and again the farmers request for the young man to tell a story and once more the young fellow refused with the words......don't know no story.

Nothing more was said on the subject and yet another week passed until once again following the morning service at the Church, and after a splendid lunch followed by a snooze, the farmer brought out the fiddle and played while his wife danced. Then before putting it away again he said to the young man "Come on what about a story, surely by now you have a story to tell. We have taken you in, given you work and treated you like a son and now we have played and danced for you is it too much to ask for a story in return?" "Don't know no story" said the disgruntled youth and with that the farmer immediately put the fiddle and bow back in its case, returned it to the back room, placed it carefully on a shelf and came back out this time holding a double barrelled shot gun which he then points at the young man and says "Right remove your boots and socks."

The youth quivering with fear somehow found the courage to question the command. Without hesitation the farmer repeated it while cocking the hammer of one of the barrels and removing the safety catch. The young man hurriedly followed the order. "Now your shirt" instructed he who held the gun. "But" said the youth. "No buts, remove your shirt demanded the farmer." The youth, accidently pulling off a couple of buttons in the process, quickly took off his collarless linen shirt and threw it in a heap on a chair. "Trousers" said the farmer "take off your trousers."

At this point in the story to uphold decency, the farmer's wife excuses herself to feed the chickens for a second time that day.

Slowly the young man unbuttoned and removed his trousers." Pants" instructed the farmer. "What, No!" replied the young man. "Not my ...." "Pants" repeated the farmer raising his gun and cocking the second barrel. "Take off your pants."

Turning his back on the farmer the young man now white as a sheet lowered and, nearly falling over as he struggled to retain at least some modesty, removed his underwear and stood there as naked as the very day he was born.

"Right" said the farmer lowering his gun. "Put your clothes back on and from this day onwards if anyone should ask you if you have a story to tell... Now you have one"

I believe I first heard a similar tale to this from the late Irish Story Teller, singer and whistle player Packie Manus Byrne, when back in the 1980s he stayed the night at mine following a Music Hall evening I had directed. I now pass my working of that story on to you.

Dildrum and Doldrum

Perhaps you my reader haven't experienced as many various types of employment as I have and maybe for good reason you wouldn't have accepted the particular one that I did some years ago.

I admit it wouldn't have been everyone's choice of work and had it been offered to your good self, you might have immediately expressed the opinion that you wouldn't be caught dead doing such a job for all the tea in China. Well, I for one haven't got the faintest idea how much tea there is in China and what's more I drink Indian; which I was doing on the night it happened.

There we were, my wife and I sitting by the fire enjoying a nice cuppa with Sylvester the cat, at our feet on the hearth rug, sprawled out on his back, paws in the air waiting for his belly to be vigorously rubbed. He was a pleasant addition to our household having adopted us a few months earlier. We had no idea where he came from, he just wandered in and made himself at home as some cats tend to do. For want of a name we called him Sylvester for no other reason than he looked like Sylvester the cartoon cat.

Snug we were that early evening while outside the wind was blowing a demented gale and the rain beat relentlessly against the window, constantly rattling a loose pane. Having got up from my well-worn but favourite armchair and while drawing the heavy curtains to subdue the draught I recall the glass domed mantelpiece clock striking the twenty-first hour as at the same time there came a loud knocking at the front door of our small comfortable thatched cottage.

"You had better go and see who that is" said my wife "Goodness knows who would want to be out on a night like this." I walked through to the hall, drew back the bolts on the door and on opening it I was almost blown over by the force of the wind which seemed to lift the drenched and amply endowed Mrs Stickler up and over the threshold into my arms.

Having disentangled myself from what was a brief, but on reflection, not an entirely unpleasant liaison, I hung her wet coat and headscarf on the back of a chair and ushered her into the warmth of the lounge. "Don't get up" she said to my wife "It's your husband I'm after." My wife gave me a sideways look. "Sorry to call round unannounced" Mrs Stickler continued "but there has arisen a bit of a problem. "Really," said my wife "and what has arisen that's caused this problem?" my wife questioned while seemingly to stare very hard in my direction.

"I was asked to come over because there has been a mistake in the diary and Richard hadn't realised until ten minutes ago." "Well can't it wait until morning?" said my wife, not at all happy that our cosy evening together should come to an abrupt end. "It's for the first thing in the morning" replied Mrs Stickler. "I don't mind" I intervened. "You be quiet" I was told by my wife who then said, "Mrs Stickler, if your fool of a husband made the mistake by not keeping track of the bookings, I suggest he goes out in this storm and does the job himself." "He can't" said our visitor, looking towards our clock, "he's now on the train for a meeting in London tomorrow and won't be back until tomorrow night. He's got a colleague to cover for him in the morning to conduct the proceedings."

By this time, I had managed to nearly get one wellington boot on. "And where do you think you are going?" demanded my nearest and dearest having seen what I was doing.

"Well, it is my job after all" I said in rather a meek tone although truthfully, I wish I had been bolder in front of Mrs Stickler; after all she was very attractive for her age. "You can go when you have finished your tea" retorted the missus "and if that will be all Mrs Stickler, we will say goodnight."

"I will see you to the door" said I. "She knows where the door is. You stay here or your tea will get cold." my wife advised me while again fixing me in a hard stare which was somewhat unnerving.

Mrs Stickler, turning on her heels but not without first giving me the most sweetest of smiles, went into the hall, put on her coat and scarf, and as she walked out into the cold windswept darkness yelled "Thank you. I'll tell Robert, next time he phones, that you will see to it. Goodnight." On the second attempt against the wind she pulled our front door shut and through the driving rain she crossed the road to where she lived.

"Come away from that window and put the curtain straight" instructed my wife. "Just seeing Philippa is safely home" I said and instantly regretted referring to our recent visitor by her Christian name. "Oh, on first name terms already then are we?" They have only been here a few weeks" my wife was quick to point out

I drank my, by now, tepid, tea in silence as Mary, for that was my wife's name, watched me intently with suspicious eyes over the top of her tortoise shell framed bi-focal glasses.

"Well I had better get on" I said having drained the last dregs of my cup in a bid to savour the remaining residue of sugar at the bottom.

Once dressed and fully booted I made myself a flask of coffee and attempted to slip, unseen, a bottle of brandy into the pocket of my waterproofs "And where do you think you are going with that" inquired Mary who was now standing cross armed in the hall doorway." "Just a drop to keep the chill at bay." I stammered. "Well, you make sure it's just a drop. Off you go then and get back, if not before, as soon after twelve as you can. I'll be waiting up for you. I want to finish my book so I can get it back to the library in the morning."

With her monotonous voice ringing in my ears I grabbed a spade and the hurricane lamp from the hall cupboard and at last I found myself outside heading towards my place of work. Luckily the wind had dropped since Philippa had left and the rain had become nothing more than a mere irritating drizzle. Such is our English weather so flighty, so unpredictable.

Crossing the road, I glanced up at the illuminated bedroom window blinds of the vicarage and in a brief moment witnessed a hazy silhouette of Philippa preparing for bed. Then looking back from where I had come, I saw my lounge curtains twitch and quickly decided not to linger but to walk on to the wrought iron gates which with cold, wet slippery hands I unlocked. Once inside I quickly establish where I thought I should put my spade, lit the lantern at the third attempt and started to dig.

Quite often while I was digging, I would mull over stories like Treasure Island or The Pedlar of Swaffham and even ponder on act five, scene one in Hamlet. But that night I had no time for such thoughts. My aim was to be done and home as quick as possible. At four or five foot down I was starting to tire, so I decided a little liquid sustenance would not go amiss. Taking the bottle from my pocket I preceded to unscrew the cap.

It was the first strike of the church bell clock announcing the midnight hour that took me completely by surprise and thereby causing me to fumble and drop the bottle. I immediately stooped down in the grave I was digging to retrieve the object and indeed the liquid of my desire. Then it was loud and clear over the sound of the doleful bell's clang I first hear, the command... "Funeral party in slow time, by the left slow march, Left Right, Left Right, Left Right Halt… Meeeow." I slowly raised my head so I could see the churchyard gate from where the sound was coming from.

I swear it was then and not a moment before that I took my first of many swigs from the bottle. There, coming towards me were six black cats up on their hind legs carrying a coffin draped with what I could make out to be some sort of royal standard on top of which was a crown. Leading the way in front of the coffin, with a military drill instructor pace stick in its paw was another cat. But this one had a white chest like our Sylvester and was wearing some sort of military cap while loudly purring the following orders. "Left Right, Left Right, Left Right halt...... Meeeow" The nearer they came the more I drank. "Left Right, Left Right, Left Right, Halt...... Meeeow" It was somewhat unnerving I can tell you especially when they stopped right beside where I was, five foot down in the ground, and the leader of this strange procession lowered his head, looked directly at me and said "Tell Dildrum that Doldrum is dead."

Well, I was up and out of that earthen hole like a shot leaving bottle, spade and lantern behind. Walking talking cats, it wasn't natural. I left that churchyard as fast as my legs would carry me and although I was reasonably fit, which was essential for the job of Grave Digger, I arrived at my front door quite exhausted. I took a moment to catch my breath and while searching my pockets for my front door key, still panting, I looked to see if the light was still on in the bedroom window across the road.

"Your door is here right behind you" I heard my wife say. I turned around to find her standing in the open doorway, arms crossed and a menacing expression on her face “I seem to have lost my key” I explained in a somewhat slurred fashion “Well its lucky I was here to open the door for you wasn't it! Get in” she said sternly “and leave your wet muddy things in the hall.”

There she left me to sort myself out while she retreated to the kitchen to fill a hot water bottle.

I propped myself up against the hall wall in an attempt to keep my balance while struggling with the zip on my outer garments; my concentration only interrupted the once by her shouting over the sound of the boiling kettle “And don't lean on the wall against the new wallpaper.” I think it was at that point that I involuntarily slid down the said wall and continued to remove my wet clothing and clay clad boots sitting on the polished wooden floor.

In slightly damp woollen socks I made slow progress into the lounge where I only just avoided tripping over Sylvester, who appeared not to have moved an inch sincc before I went out. I slumped into my armchair next to a now cold empty grate.

“Well” said my wife coming into the room “did you get the grave dug before you decided against my wishes to drink yourself silly into a drunken stupor?”

“You would have done the same if you had seen what I have seen... anyway I'm not drunk” I said, “I only had a drop.” “More than a drop by the state of you. I was saving that brandy for the Christmas pudding and where's the bottle?” she retorted.

Being full of Dutch courage I continued to speak, to tell my story, but by the time I had got to the point of what the cat with the white chest had said to me the wife had gone up the stairs, thrown down some bedding and slammed the bedroom door with the words “What a lot of rubbish, I'm fed up with your stories especially when you've had a few too many drinks. You won't be sleeping up here tonight you drunken old fool.”

I looked down at Sylvester and said “Well then, Sylvester it looks like it's just you and me. You never argue so I'll tell you what the cat with the white chest like yours said” and while rubbing Sylvester's chest I repeated the words “Tell Dildrum that Doldrum is dead.”

In an instant Sylvester was up on hind legs. “Don't call me Sylvester. I hate the name Sylvester. Dildrum” he said “that's my real name and now with Doldrum dead that makes me King of the Cats. I'm off.” With that he then shot up the chimney and was gone without a word of thanks.

I was roused the next morning by an urgent knocking at the door. “I'll answer that” called out my wife while coming down the stairs.

I heard the front door open and heard my wife say “Good morning, I saw you from upstairs coming across the road. How can I help you?” “It's your husband I would like a word with”, replied the distinct voice of Mrs Philippa Stickler. “There's been an awful mistake over in the graveyard and I want your husband to go over there straight away and put it right. In the dark he obviously didn't realise where he was digging. It would seem he has dug into another's grave.”

When I arrived at the grave which I'd dug the previous night I immediately saw the problem. There was already a coffin in there and next to it the brandy bottle. Not only that, very soon a funeral cortege was due to arrive outside the gates. It was a small coffin, so I decided to remove it and conceal it behind some bushes until the other coffin just arriving, could be lowered, with due reverence and the service performed. Concluding with, hopefully the relatives and friends quickly departing the scene for the wake. Then I could retrieve the other coffin put in on top, back fill the grave, and no one would be the wiser.

I climbed down into the pit I'd dug, and it was then I read the brass plate on the coffin lid. DOLDRUM.

Apparently, the visiting celebrant, prone to partake of tobacco, having a quick smoke and a wander around the graveyard before greeting the large number of mourners gathering outside the gates, discovered me sprawled out over Doldrum's coffin holding the empty brandy bottle and gibbering like an idiot in-between Meowing like a cat.

I am getting treatment now and no longer being employed it just about gave me time, between frequent visits from Phillipa, to write this story.

My slant on a normally very short English folk tale 'King of the Cats'.

We Are What We Are

He had just eaten an absolutely wonderfully scrumptiously delicious lunch. And now he sat in his soft cosy armchair fast asleep with his face hidden beneath the Rodent Times, a newspaper he had been reading, that rose up and down in a flutter as he snored.

"Mr Mouse, Mr Mouse" came the voice of Mrs Mouse from the Kitchen. Mr Mouse continued to sleep and snore and snored some more. Snore, snore, snore.

"Mr Mouse, I hope you're not asleep" shouted Mrs Mouse while drying up the dinner plates and putting them tidily away into a kitchen cupboard "I want you to go to the supermarket." From Mr Mouse, other than his snoring there was not a sound, not a peep. He snored, and snored and stayed asleep, the result of counting sheep after sheep. Snore, snore, snore.

Mrs Mouse came to the kitchen doorway and shouted "Mr Mouse" as loud as she could. Her husband very slowly lowered the newspaper, just a little, and peered over the top. "Yes" he said then went back to sleep and snored and snored and snored some more.

His wife came into the room and snatched away the newspaper and gave her husband a jolly good shake saying "Come on lazy bones we are out of cheese. I want you to go down the road and get some more." "I would rather not" said Mr Mouse having now woken up. "Why ever not?" said Mrs Mouse. "I'm scared" he replied, "You see" he continued "everything outside our green front door is so very big and I am so very small." "Oh don't be so silly, who's going take any notice of you. Come on up you get and off you go." Mr Mouse reluctantly got out of his soft cosy arm chair and went into the hall where he put on his hat and coat. “Don't forget your scarf” said his wife wrapping round his neck a brightly coloured piece of material they had found near a sewing box. “It's quite chilly outside today. Now off you go and don't forget what you are going for.” Mr Mouse gave a vague look. “Cheese” she reminded him.

Mr Mouse gingerly opened the green front door; then as if he was about to cross a road, he first looked to his left, then to his right, then left again, after which he stepped out onto the pavement and very hesitantly started to walk towards the Supermarket. The further he went the more confident he became. With each step his anxiety diminished and everything appeared to be fine. All seemed well with the world. That is until he went around the corner. On seeing what he then saw he shrieked “Aghhhhh” and dashed back down the pavement past his green front door and over the rickety bridge to where the Wizard lived.

He knocked hard, three times, on the wizard's door. Bang, Bang, Bang. Then, creaking and squeaking just like any other wizard's door, it slowly opened and there stood the wizard just like any other wizard.

He had a long white beard and wore a tall pointed hat and a long blue gown on which were embroidered the stars in fine silver thread and the moon in gold. In one hand he held a magic wand and in the other a jam sandwich which he had yet to take a bite of.

I think at this point of the story it's only fair to point out to you my reader that this is, if you hadn't already guessed, mainly a story for children and that wizards don't normally eat jam sandwiches when answering their front door. Although they do quite often have an owl perched on their shoulder, I thought it wasn't practical to include one due to the fact that owls eat mice and this story would be well and truly over no sooner had it began.

"Yes," said the wizard looking down at Mr Mouse. "How can I help you?"

"Well" replied Mr Mouse "I wondered if you could change me into something bigger. You see I'm so very small and everyone and everything is so much larger than me. I get very scared." "And what would you have me change you into?" inquired the wizard "Remember we are what we are and if I change you into something different, I can never change you back again"

Mr Mouse started to think, and he thought, and he thought and thought some more then said "Cat. Yes, can you please change me into a cat? A cat is bigger than a mouse so if I were a cat I wouldn't be scared. Please Mr Wizard, please change me into a cat" "Very well" said the wizard but remember. "We are what we are and if I change you into a cat, I can never change you back again"

"I don't care" said Mr Mouse hastily. The wizard then, waving his Magic wand, created a gentle sprinkle of bright sparkling star dust and there, where had stood a mouse now stood a cat.

The cat went "Meow", then stuck its tail in the air, by way of saying thank you, as it crossed the rickety bridge and went off down the street. Everything appeared to be fine and all seemed well with the world. That is, until he went around the corner and on seeing what he saw he shrieked "Aghhhhh" and dashed back down the pavement pass Mr Mouse's green front door and over the rickety bridge to where the Wizard lived.

He knocked hard, three times on the wizard's door. Bang, Bang, Bang. Then, creaking and squeaking just like any other wizard's door, it slowly opened and there stood the wizard just like any other wizard with his long white beard and wearing a tall pointed hat and a long blue gown on which were embroidered the stars in fine silver thread and the moon in gold. In one hand he still held his magic wand and in the other the jam sandwich which he still had not yet taken a bite of.

"Yes," said the Wizard "What can I do for you?" "Well" replied the cat who was once a mouse. I wondered if you could change me into something bigger. "And what would you have me change you into?" said the wizard "Remember we are what we are and if I change you into something larger, I can never change you back again." Then, the cat who was once a mouse started to think and he thought, and he thought, and he thought some more then said "A dog, can you please change me into a dog because a dog is bigger than a cat. Therefore, if I were a dog I wouldn't be scared. Please Mr Wizard please change me into a dog." "Very well," said the Wizard but remember we are what we are and if I change you into a dog, I can never change you back again." "I don't care" said the cat hastily. The wizard then, waving his Magic wand, created a gentle sprinkle of bright sparkling star dust and there, where had stood a cat that was once a mouse now stood a dog that went "Woof" and wagged its tail by way of saying thank you as it crossed the rickety bridge and went off down the street. Everything appeared to be fine and all seemed well with the world. That is until he went around the corner and on seeing what he saw he shrieked "Aghhhhh" and dashed back down the pavement past Mr Mouse's green front door and over the rickety bridge to where the Wizard lived.

He knocked hard three times on the wizard's door. Bang, Bang, Bang. Then, creaking and squeaking just like any other wizard's door, it slowly opened and there stood the wizard, just like any other wizard with his long white beard and wearing a tall pointed hat and a long blue gown on which were embroidered the stars in fine silver thread and the moon in gold. In one hand he still held his magic wand and in the other the jam sandwich which he still hadn't taken a bite of. Not even a nibble.

"Yes," said the Wizard to the dog. "What can I do for you?" "Well" replied the dog who was once a cat, who was once a mouse "I wondered if you could change me into something bigger." "And what would you have me change you into?" replied the wizard "Remember we are what we are and if I change you into something larger, I can never change you back again." Then, the dog who was once a cat, who was once a mouse started to think and he thought, and he thought, and he thought some more then said "A cow, can you please change me into a cow because a cow is bigger than a dog? Therefore, if I were a cow I wouldn't be scared. Please Mr Wizard please change me into a cow." "Very well", said the Wizard "but remember what I said. We are what we are and if I change you into a cow, I can never change you back again." "I don't care" said the dog hastily. The wizard then, waving his Magic wand, created a gentle sprinkle of bright sparkling star dust and there, where had stood a dog who was once a cat, who was once a mouse now stood a Cow that went "Moo" as it flicked its tail by way of saying thank you, and crossed the rickety bridge and went off down the street.

Everything appeared to be fine and all seemed well with the world until that is, she went around the corner and on seeing what she saw she shrieked "Aghhhhh" and dashed back down the pavement past Mr Mouse's green front door and over the rickety bridge to where the Wizard lived. She knocked hard three times on the wizard's door. Bang, Bang, Bang. Then creaking and squeaking just like any other wizard's door it slowly opened and there stood the wizard just like any other wizard with his long white beard and wearing a tall pointed hat and a long blue gown on which were embroidered the stars in fine silver thread and the moon in gold. In one hand he still held his magic wand and in the other the jam sandwich. Still not having had the chance to sit down and have a bite of that sandwich or even the slightest lick he was getting very hungry plus a little angry. "Yes," said the Wizard to the cow "What can I do for you now?" "Well" replied the cow who was once a dog who was once a cat who was once a mouse.

"I wondered if you could change me into something bigger." "And what would you have me change you into?" said the wizard "Remember we are what we are and if I change you into something larger, I can never change you back again."

Then, the cow who was once a dog, who was once a cat, who was once a mouse started to think and he thought, and he thought, and he thought some more then said "A horse. Can you please change me into a horse? A horse is bigger than a cow. Therefore, if I were a horse I wouldn't be scared. Please Mr Wizard please change me into a horse." "Very well," said the Wizard but remember what I said. We are what we are, and I can never change you back again." "I don't care" said the cow hastily. The wizard then, waving his Magic wand, created a gentle sprinkle of bright sparkling star dust and there, where had stood a cow now stood a horse that went "Neigh " as it raised its tail and by way of saying thank you, left a large present on the path for the wizard's garden then crossed the rickety bridge and went off down the street.

Everything was fine and all seemed well with the world until that is, he went around the corner and on seeing what he saw he shrieked "Aghhhhh" and dashed back down the pavement past Mr Mouse's green front door and over the rickety bridge to where the Wizard lived.

The horse didn't knock three times on the Wizards door; there was no need. It was still wide open because the poor wizard hadn't had the chance to shut it by the time the horse came galloping back. On its arrival it slipped on the parcel it had so generously left behind on the path. Transporting the wizard with it, the horse skidded down the hall, through the kitchen to the patio and then stopped abruptly; and in doing so tossed the wizard over the crumbling garden wall.

The wizard was not now looking just like any other wizards do (unless of course you my reader know of wizards who have jam sandwiches stuck to their beard and wear squashed and bent pointed hats as well as torn and ragged dirt covered blue cloaks with hardly an embroidered star or moon visible anywhere).

Getting up, the poor bruised and dishevelled wizard hauled himself back over the garden wall and very angrily shouted at the horse. “Before you ask, let me guess. You want to be changed into something bigger. Well how about this!” Then frantically the wizard waved the two pieces of his now broken magic wand producing an enormous deluge of star dust and there, where had first stood a mouse, then a cat, then a dog, then a cow, then a horse now stood the biggest elephant you my patient reader is ever likely to see. Huge it was with massive flapping ears, two long white ivory tusks and a long trunk that looked as though it could, like a giant vacuum cleaner, suck up anything in its path. “Now go away and leave me alone” bellowed the wizard and slammed his door shut, without a creak or a squeak but with one big loud BANG. The elephant who was totally confused and taken aback by the wizard’s attitude retorted “Goodness me, I will never forget such a rude and angry wizard.”

The elephant then didn't cross the rickety bridge but because of its weight, unfortunately, it smashed it to smithereens and then continued wet footed, down the street.

Just as it got to the green door where Mr Mouse had lived, Mrs Mouse looked out to see where her husband had got to. “Aghhhhh” shrieked the elephant and stood there in the street trembling, shaking and quaking because even as big as they are the thing that an elephant is scared of is a mouse. And the only thing us husbands are scared of is... our wives.

I'm not sure if and where I heard a similar story, it just seemed to become part of my repertoire and evolved with each telling. The detail even more so on the printed page.

The concept that elephants are afraid of mice, because while an elephant sleeps a mouse can climb up inside its trunk and send it crazy, is based on a myth dating as far back as the ancient Greeks.

Churchie Deal

"Roll-up, Roll-up for all the fun fair." Ned was in his element standing there in his brown bowler hat and his patriotic striped waistcoat yelling through his highly polished brass megaphone which he had purchased the day before from Davey and Co of London for this once a year occasion.

"Coconut Shy sir? Over there beside the fence. Crazy Kitchen lads? There right behind you" he instructed.

A year had passed since, while buttering a scone in the dusty, musty smelling tea tent, poor old Tom dropped down dead. Most people were truly shocked and saddened at Tom's sudden demise especially as he hadn't had a chance to taste his recent purchase the like of which were said to have been particularly delicious that year.

However, not all were as deeply affected and quick to mourn Tom's passing as was the case with Ned who for many years had concealed his envy of Tom's position as Master of Ceremonies at the St Clements Church May Fair.

Still, now with old Tom pushing up daisies there had appeared an immediate vacancy which Ned had been only too happy and quick to fill. Here at last was his chance to excel in front of his fellow parishioners and he took to it with flamboyant gusto.

"Roll for a pig, thrupence a go; all in a good cause" he heartily yelled through his loud hailer; causing a young lady, passing close by, to shriek in flustered alarm and drop her dainty lace parasol in a muddy puddle, evidence of an early morning downpour forgotten by most people now the day was warm with the sun brightly shining on them and their endeavours to exceed the previous year's record for raising money towards church funds.

While the majority of parishioners were across the way in Rectory meadows enjoying the parochial festivities (and having securely locked the church for the day) the Sexton was determined to spend his own leisure time at home in his potting shed with his beloved geraniums with no intention whatsoever of re-opening God's house again until the next day.

"Roll up, Roll up for all the fun of the Fair. Great views of the Estuary from the swing boats" informed Ned as he trod on the parasol in his haste to be seen standing next to some local dignitary on the other side of the field who was preparing to have his photograph taken.

As flags gently fluttered in the breeze and the village band struck up a tune for the freshly scrubbed children of the local school to give a ribbon weaving dance display around the May Pole, Ned (suddenly realising he was in the wrong place at the wrong time) ran for all his worth back across the now well-trodden grass to announce the display and on arrival got himself entangled in a loose ribbon that some child refused to hold.

Now far too late for the actual start of the colourful event, and against a teacher's advice, Ned was persistent that he should still announce the energetic youthful show. So, puffing and blowing he proceeded with his introduction "Ladies and Gentlemen, a big round of applause please for the boys and girls of our much-admired local School May Pole Team dancing to the tune Princess Royal" "Oh do shut up you silly old fool" said an irritated father who was watching the show. "You are too late. Can't you see they are already dancing. You've missed your cue. No one can hear you anyway over the sound of the band except me and that's because your brass trumpet thingy is virtually in my ear hole. It's about time someone rammed that bloody horn down your throat or somewhere else where the sun don't shine." Either Ned didn't hear him, or he just chose to ignore the remark as he rushed off to rub shoulders with the Bishop who had just arrived amidst a loud round of applause in congratulation for yet another book he'd just had published. Needless to say, he had brought with him a considerable number of copies to sell which he was also willing to sign for an extra fee to go towards the historical church fabric fund.

However, what you my loyal reader have already digested I'm afraid has little or nothing to do with the story that I now intend to relate other than loosely creating a backdrop to the scene which I will now unfold.

It was while all this joviality was going on in the church meadow that a separate drama of a sinister nature was being played out around the church itself. A family of travellers had arrived with the intention, while the good people of the parish were distracted, to break into the ancient building and to steal from the alms box as well as remove anything else which might be small enough to carry but worth a few bob when sold.

In the main there's nothing wrong with travelling folk. I myself am of gypsy stock having been conceived amidst pots and pans and dolly pegs in a shadowed space within a traditional horse drawn Bow Top wagon. There's good and bad in all walks of life; of that I'm sure you my reader will agree.

Anyway, with that said this band of pilferers, having found the door to be securely locked but confident that they hadn't been seen, encouraged a small boy in their company to scramble up the rampant ivy, which profusely clung to the Kentish rag stone tower, to where slightly concealed among the shiny green leaves and hairy vine there was a tiny window off its latch and slightly ajar.

Having gained entry the boy encountered, for his size, a considerable drop from the sill to the tower's stone tread worn spiral staircase. And as he lowered himself, he heard from outside the megaphone voice of Ned shouting "Gypsies over there at the church, Gypsies, bloody Gypsies."

The band of marauding thieves were quickly chased off while Ned stood proudly. unashamedly, bathing in the praise being bestowed upon him for his observation skills and his swift decisive action.

With the incident seemingly over, those fair-goers who had given chase went back to the festivities while the boy, said to be about six or seven years of age, gingerly made his way down to the bottom of the staircase only to be confronted by a stout iron hinged oak door which was locked. Knowing that he was too small to reach the window and go back out the way he'd come in, he sat on the cold bottom step and sobbed. What creepy and terrifying thoughts and visions that poor lad must have experienced alone in the darkness we can only imagine.

It was next morning when the Sexton, on opening the church in preparation for the Sunday service, first heard the sound of whimpering which he initially dismissed as the wind periodically entering through broken roof tiles which the previous day's event was partly in aid of raising funds to repair. However, on further investigation he realised that the noises where in fact coming from behind the tower door. Opening the said door, to his amazement he discovered the boy cowering and shivering on the step behind. By this time the Sunday morning worshipers had, in dribs and drabs, started to arrive and were all equally amazed at the situation and were likewise keen to voice their opinion as to what should be done with the young lad, who on being questioned as to who he was and where he had come from would only, between tearful sobs and bouts of anguished crying, mumble the word "Deal."

Even after a nice warm drink and a biscuit or two no further information was forth coming, so many immediately assumed he came from the small coastal town of Deal in Kent. The presiding incumbent, who had missed most of the proceedings having entered the church through the vestry door and immediately robed himself in his vestments of the day, suggested the boy should be placed in care at the workhouse orphanage in a neighbouring parish. There didn't seem to be any further ideas put forward other than to hand the child over to the local constabulary, a suggestion which didn't sit well with the benevolent nature of the majority of those people from down the hill in the old town who made up the congregation that morning, so the rector's proposal was accepted and following the service preparations were made to transport the young lad to the sometimes harsh residential institution of a children's home.

With the sexton's arrival with a pony and trap, hired from the local coaching Inn, proceedings were brought to a sudden halt by the altogether timely intervention of a charitable Leigh fishing family of good standing in the community who offered to take the youngster in and bring him up as one of their own.

And so it was, the young waif was absorbed into that Leigh family and the Thames side village community as one of their own and being so, like many others of that hamlet by the sea he became known by a nickname and his was 'Churchie'. Churchie Deal, on account he was found in the church (and as I have already mentioned) it was thought by many that he came from that place name in Kent- even though back in those days, travelling by roads which were often deeply rutted, it was a hundred and more miles away. But that's the old fishing folk for you. They only tend to see things nautically. To them Deal was just a boat trip south east across the river and around the north foreland of Thanet then south down the coast to Deal.

However, it's more plausible that the frightened and sobbing gypsy child was relating his surname as Dill which was a recognised gypsy family surname among the British nomadic fraternity.

But whatever, I'm sure you my loyal reader will be pleased to know that Churchie, appeared to have lived to a ripe old age when in 1913 he was laid to rest and there are families in Leigh to this day who are his descendants.

Based on an old (disputed) Leigh story told by the late Sheila Pitt Stanley.

Claude the Gentleman Dragon

It was Autumn and I was taking a brisk energetic walk along the narrow high hedged winding lanes of east Sussex. At one point I conversed with a snail, as one does, as it slowly silvered the path I was travelling. "Catch up" I said. "Slow down, slow down not everyone can travel at your speed nor wants to" said the snail. A slight breeze ruffled the gold and amber leaves on the trees as though in agreement. "You see that?" said the snail "Not one leaf fell, not one, neither will it until its appointed time; a time laid down by Mother Nature herself. The wind is constantly trying to unclothe the tree, but it stands firm and will not disrobe and lay itself bare again until it is ready within the pre-ordained grand order of things. Slow down, slow down. What is to be will be. Night will follow day as day will follow night."

I thanked him for his advice and found myself content to watch him for an hour or more until he had travelled the short distance to a stone and disappear from view just as a young buck rabbit bounded past and fell headlong into a ditch in a flurry of displaced fur.

I continued my journey, slower than before, allowing myself time to mull over in my mind a story to tell my little friend Hugo when I arrived at his home. Then, just as I was about to round one of the many bends in the lane, I suddenly felt a searing heat, as a red ball of fire shot past and upwards to disperse in a cloud of smoke above my head.

"Awfully sorry about that old chap." came a voice from behind a bush on the other side of the narrow road "Dashed bad luck. Didn't see you coming. I do so apologise, very remiss of me. You should whistle a tune, a little ditty or something when travelling the highways and byways of fair Albion. Old name for Britain. Much more poetic. Got more of a ring to it don't you think? Yes, whistle or sing a song if you are so inclined and then us Dragons will know you are coming. Far better that way. No chance of accidents. Health and Safety and all that. You didn't have a beard, did you?"

From behind the scorched grass bank where I had unceremoniously flung myself into a ditch, I slowly edged my way back to cautiously peer across the lane. "Come on, up you jump old boy" continued the unseen owner of the voice. "Let's shake hand and claw and be friends. Too much trouble in this world already. Why add to it!"

Then all of a sudden before you could say pig piggy squeak, there, in the middle of a quiet ordinary English country lane, stood a smartly, if not a little over dressed, Dragon in pinstriped suit, bow tie, bowler hat, a monocle to his eye and supporting, neatly tucked beneath his wing, a furled umbrella. "Well don't just stand there mouth wide open old chap" he said, "too many flies about this time of day, all right if you are a frog or maybe you were once until a princess made a mistake and gave you a kiss." He started to laugh "Just a dragon joke, no offence meant, none whatsoever. Come, let me formally introduce myself."

"I must have bumped my head" I said shaking it a couple of times from side to side in disbelief at what I was seeing. "You appear to be a D r a g o n" I eventually managed to say. "Very observant of you dear fellow." came the reply with what I sensed to be a slight hint of sarcasm. "Yes, I am a Dragon and jolly proud of it too I can tell you. Claude's the name." "But" I said, "With the greatest of respect, you are not at all how I imagined a dragon to look" "And how should a Dragon look?" he retorted "Too smart for you am I? Is that it, too good looking? I pride myself on my good looks you know. Well how about this old bean." he chuckled and immediately transformed into the most fearful hideous dark murky coloured beast of his type which I never thought I could possibly imagine. "Well is this more what you had in mind" he snarled, viciously stabbing at the air in my direction with long razor-sharp claws. "Or maybe this" he said, immediately changing into a dragon of the red variety "This is my Welsh number boy'o, and this Laddie", changing to green, "my Scottish look. And what about this one" he continued changing, this time to white as he spoke the words. "I never do the red and white one directly after each other, always tend to find that I am at odds with myself but you know all about that don't you Merlin?"

"Pardon," I said thinking that I had misheard him. "Merlin" he repeated. No, I had not been mistaken. "That is your name is it not?" he questioned, as his narrow eyes pierced mine through to the innermost core of my deepest thoughts. My mouth became parched as I felt a lump well up in my throat as a tear of past memories trickled slowly down my cheek. "I have been called such," I admitted "but that was a long, long time ago when a cuddly toy dragon lived in the brightly painted toy box at the foot of my bed. We grew up together. He was always part of my games and helping to inspire my imagination. Heady childhood days when anything and everything became just whatever I wanted it to be, as we ventured to dance among the stars and play football with the moon. So long, so long, so very long ago now."

"Jolly hockey sticks I thought it was you." said Claude reverting back to his former dragon self in pin stripes with, I noticed this time, a red carnation in the button hole of his jacket." "It's you, it's you" he shouted with excitement. A few leaves gently floated to the ground.

Now, when a Dragon whispers it is very loud but when a Dragon shouts, well.... "Yes" I yelled in an effort to be heard "I am Merlin." More leaves fluttered earthward. Claude the dragon was by now in what I understood to be some sort of joyful celebration dance and I thought it only polite to join in. Round and round we twirled as russet leaves fell about us like soft confetti.

Suddenly Claude stopped his frantic movements, put his head to one side inquiringly and said, "Is that how you do it?" "Oh yes" I replied more confused by his antics than impressed but all the same not wishing to hurt his feelings. "You dance very well" I told him. "Dance? Dance? I was not dancing." he scowled. "I was trying to fly."

The tree was now stripped of its last flimsy garment and stood once more naked. The season's cycle was complete. "Will you teach me how to fly, Merlin?" His voice had changed, taken on a softer tone, an echo from my past, "You have the power that inspires me and gives me confidence to soar like a bird high above my own self-doubt." "I would never have taken you for someone to lack confidence" I said, truly surprised by this revelation. "Oh, I do" he replied, his eyes now lowered, staring at the ground. "All this changing character to suit other's idea of me, the continuous joviality, it's really all just a sham, a mask. I have always had wings as we all have if we use our imagination, but I have never been taught how to use them." "I assure you" I said "it's not imagination alone, but also courage. The courage, and the will to follow your deep inner feelings. If you find the courage to be your true self, then you will indeed fly."

The wind swirled the fallen leaves as the evening's first star gave bright new lustre to the diminishing pale autumn sky. "By Jove, Merlin you are so right. Thank you., thank you so very, very much for that advice, a most wonderful gift" said my dragon companion, and then jumping up and down with great excitement he exclaimed

"I feel like a heavy weight has been lifted from me. But when Merlin, when will I fly?" he then inquired. "In time" I replied, "In time your whole self will follow where your spirit, your heart and mind together truly lead." "Heart?' he said in perplexed amazement" "But I'm a dragon, Dragon's don't have a heart." "Oh yes they do... somewhere." I reassured him.

"Thank you again Merlin old chap you really do still have the power. The imagination" he said "Yes" I admitted sheepishly "I suppose I do, although for a long time until now, I was convinced I had lost such a precious and treasured jewel."

Out of the now darkened sky a wishing star fell to earth leaving its trail, for a brief moment suspended like a canopy high above the bed of fallen auburn leaves. I stood transfixed, staring deep, in a vain attempt to penetrate the very core of the star buttoned heavens. "I had better be on my way." I said reluctantly. "The hour is late and my journey long." "But I have given you nothing in return for your gift to me" said Claude anxiously. "I did not give in order to receive." I told him. "That's all very well old boy but even so it would be dashed bad form if I didn't reciprocate your kindness in some small way. Now what can I do for you", he mused out load.

I then ducked as a column of fire erupted from his mouth and lit up the night sky "Oops, sorry about that" he said, rubbing his belly with his claw "I should have warned you. A bout of indigestion that's all, nothing to fear." "That's it, that's it" I exclaimed. "Would you teach me how to breathe and eat fire?" "Gladly" said my country lane host removing his monocle and giving it a quick wipe with a swipe of his tail. "However, there are certain conditions that you must promise to abide by." he continued in the now authoritarian voice of a school teacher. Indeed, he was now wearing the cloak and cap of that profession and had from somewhere quickly procured a blackboard on which he wrote the following in large bold letters. **ONE:** WARN CHILDREN THEY MUST NEVER PLAY WITH FIRE BECAUSE IT'S VERY DANGEROUS. **TWO:** NEVER TELL ANYONE HOW THE TRICK IS DONE. **THREE**: ALWAYS GET PAID WELL WHEN PERFORMING WITH FIRE. **FOUR:** MAKE SURE YOU ARE WELL INSURED. The smell of chalk as it squeaked its way across the blackened surface instantly transported my thoughts back through time to the happy idyllic schooldays of my childhood; opening my mind's eye like the open window of my old classroom from where I looked out far beyond the freshly mown grass of the playing fields on which the stumps and bails were already in place awaiting the quite often erratic aim of a young bowler's arm. Far up and away, I travelled over the ripe golden-eared barley to where the tall white bellowing clouds created a logical playground for my fantasies. “Pay attention there,” came my teachers voice as a piece of chalk struck me not too softly behind the ear. “Yes Sir.” I answered automatically. I couldn’t afford to be kept behind after school today, for there were Gunfights to be fought in the O.K Corral. Treasure to be won on the high seas of the Spanish Main, the olive grove coast of the Mediterranean and..... “Merlin! Merlin!” The words seemed distant at first, then slowly become clearer more audible. “Merlin, Merlin. My dear fellow” said Claude “Have you not taken in anything I've been saying?” “I’m sorry, Claude.” I said somewhat embarrassed by my quite obvious slip of concentration.

The remainder of that night was filled with the greatest excitement mixed with, I have to admit, a little trepidation as Claude the Gentleman Dragon taught me from his vast experience all there was to know about eating and breathing fire. “There you are old bean.” said Claude as night's dark veil was drawing back to make way for the pallor of a morning sky “I've taught you all I know, I can teach you no more and here is a tube of cream for that burn.” “Thank you”, I said. “Not at all,” said my friend 'it was my pleasure, but I must leave now. I have a toy box to go to. You must pop by and say hello. If you are passing, that is.” “I shall do that.” I told him.

“Merlin,” said Claude. His voice dropping to a low nervous whisper. “Merlin, I know this might sound a little strange, a little odd what with you being grown up and all that but…” “What is it?” I said knowingly reassuring, to save him further agitation. “Will you kiss me?” came the shy request. “Of course” I replied and without hesitation I kissed him lightly on the brow.

“I never imagined a real Dragon to be so friendly” I said. “Friendly, soft and cuddly that's me” echoed Claude's distant response.

Two stars, like eyes, shimmered simultaneously in the northern sky then slowly disappeared engulfed in the brightness of a new dawn.

When, later that morning I eventually arrived at the home of my niece in Sussex her two-year-old auburn-haired son Hugo was already up and delving into his toy box at the end of his bed looking for the soft cuddly toy dragon I had given him on one of my many visits.

The essence of this story has taken on many forms for many reasons since I first wrote it but now this final version I dedicate to Hugo.

'Two stars like eyes shimmered simultaneously in the northern sky' refers to the stars Eltanin and Rastaban in the constellation of Draco the Dragon.

Dream Not of Tomorrow

Dream not of tomorrow
While today is still a dream of yesterday
Dream not of tomorrow
While today is still a dream away

See the mist around the tor
Merlin standing boldly before
Listening for the dragon's roar
At the break of day

Chorus

The mighty oak now autumn brown
Soon the holly will bear the crown
For a king of high renown
At the break of day

Chorus

See the star as forsworn
A diadem, a jewel in the dawn
Proclaiming Uther's son is born
At the break of day

Chorus

The child is taken without delay
And wisdom taught a wizard's way
A babe, that some would wish to slay
At the break of day

Chorus

Now see before you an anvil stone
In it a sword for a king to own
And standing there a youth alone
At the break of day

Chorus

He takes the hilt he draws the blade
A king is crowned, a legend made
Hern stands silent in the glade
At the break of day

Chorus

Grasp the chalice glinting bright
A horn of plenty, a mystic rite
And you too shall have the sight
At the break of day

Chorus

Spins the table like a wheel
Now out of touch with what is real
As another comes to impose his will
At the break of day

Chorus

Spring breaks forth from winters hold
As the prophet had foretold
Two dragons fight, now one more bold
At the break of day

Chorus

The seasons cycle is now done
The cuckoos flown, summers come
The oak supreme, the battle won
At the break of day

Chorus

The mist has lifted, the dreams no more
Merlin sleeps beneath the tor
Avalon's barge has left the shore
At the break of day

Chorus

I wrote this song in 1993 for an outdoor production with Four Seasons Events the premier

Craft Fair Organisers of their day for whom I performed over many years as Fire-Eater, Stilt-Walker, Musician and much more besides.

The Death of King Arthur.

(the true story… well sort of)

Always thought to be invincible Arthur King of All Britain now lay dying. From dawn to dusk the battle had raged with no quarter asked for and none given. It had been a hard-fought battle but now it was over. The usurper Mordred the king's bastard son was dead and firmly skewered to the ground with a lance through his neck, driven home by his father's own hand. Mordred, born of Morgana, Arthur's half-sister, now stripped of his armour and undergarments, lay face down in the sticky hoof-churned earth where pitiless marauding camp following scavenging women had left him among the other slain and dying.

The smell of sweat betrayed the fear of those injured who desperately tried to hold on to life's breath as the pillaging band of dark cowled crones stepped among them gleefully brandishing their dispatching tool. These women were keen eyed and could see the slightest of movement at fifty paces. Then it was quick, if not painless, as a grubby blood-stained hand raised a knight's visor and with a Rodel dagger as slim, as sharp and as pointed as a bodkin, she would calmly, without hesitation, skewer straight into a victim's eye and upwards to the portals of the brain.

But now all was still, all was silent. No more the cries of anguish, the shrieks of pain. The merciless women, rich with ill gained possessions, the spoils of war had left the field of battle to the ghostly spirits of the old and young ravaged corpses; as a mist, like a mourner's veil, descended over the gruesome scene.

The mortally wounded Arthur aided by his loyal knight Bedivere had avoided such a gruesome end. His crown was still firmly upon his royal head and his sword Excalibur in his hand as he lay protected in a concealed hollow beside the lake from where in his youth, those many years ago, the magical weapon had been bestowed upon him by Nimue the Lady of that Lake. However, now was the time for the sword to be returned to those shadowy waters surrounding the mystical Isle of Avalon.

Not having the strength to stand and walk to the water's edge and cast the weapon far out into the lake himself, Arthur requested his sole companion to do the deed for him.

Taking the sword, Bedivere made his way down to the shore. The weight of it alone proved it could only belong to and have been wielded in battle by, the true and rightful King of Britain, Arthur Pendragon son of Uther. As Bedivere summoned all his strength and held Excalibur high above his head in preparation to cast it far out into the dark depths of the lake, a shaft of sunlight broke through the swirling mist, bouncing and separating beams of light like a cosmic star from off the silvered blade while at the same time illuminating the numerous precious jewels deeply set into the sword's pommel, to gleam and brightly sparkle in the eyes of the faithful old knight.

Standing there alone Bedivere reasoned that his dying liege, lord and friend had, due to his wounds become delirious, and to throw the mighty sword into the lake would be nothing but foolishness. So, with that in mind he hid Excalibur beneath a flowering thorn bush and returned to Arthur.

"Thank you" said Arthur "you are a good and loyal friend. I would have loved to have witnessed what you have just seen" "Seen my Lord?" questioned Bedivere "I saw nothing but the sword hitting the water and then sink from sight." "Then you have not done my bidding said Arthur between gasps of pain. "Go again to the shore and do as I command."

Not wanting to defy his king a second time Bedivere went back to the lakeside with all good intention of fulfilling the royal order. However, having taken the sword from where he had hidden it under the bush of thorns, he once again found he could not dispose of such a priceless object as his King had commanded and again concealed it beneath the bush and went back to the dying monarch.

"Now tell me truthfully" said the King weakly, as life's thin silver thread was ever nearer to leaving the royal body and with it take Arthur's soul to heaven. "What did you see when you threw the sword Excalibur into the lake. "I saw a shaft of light that broke through the mist and glinted with the brightness of a star upon the blade before it touched the wetness of the lake and vanished from my sight. That is all my Lord" replied Bedivere.

Arthur slowly and painfully raised himself up on one elbow and with all his strength and between pauses to cough up blood, he rebuked the knight kneeling before him saying "You lie. You my Marshall, my oldest friend, have deceived me and by doing so denied me my last wish on this earth in order to feed your own greed. You are no better than the camp followers that rob from the mutilated bodies of the dead and dying even the smallest of glinting trinkets that might prove of some worth. Is it not enough that I was deceived by Guinevere and Lancelot? Was not this battle fought to uphold honour and truth; the very principles of the Round Table? And was not Camelot built on those very same foundations?" "Sire" remorsefully sobbed the errant knight "Please forgive me for not doing as you commanded. It was not for gain but in the belief that such a weapon and its power should be saved for the good and prosperity of all Britain." "Then do as I bid you" replied Arthur so that generation after generation might know the truthful end to this story."

Bedivere returned again to the shingle beach and once more having retrieved the precious sword he stood for a moment gazing in sheer wonder not only at the inlaid precious stones but also the fine craftsmanship of the blade on which was inscribed the words TAKE ME UP AND CAST ME AWAY.

He read the words out loud (as I request you my reader to also do) and as he did so the mist rose like a curtain upon a stage and the sword felt lighter in his hand. Leaning back, he hurled Excalibur far out over the waters to the centre of the lake where it remained suspended above the surface shimmering amidst a radiant beam of light.

Then to the sound of heavenly music, from the depths of that lake there appeared a female leg. Then another, making a pair. Then another pair and then another until there were eight pairs of legs complete with feet and toes gracefully gliding through the rippling water in a circle below the sword. Round and round they went. First this way, then that way. Sometimes, together dipping below the surface and reappearing one leg at a time.

Bedivere sat upon a rock transfixed by what he was seeing. Slowly the music built to a climax and as it did so, in unison, all pairs of feet wiggled their toes and came together around the jewelled hilt of the sword. With the tune's finale note, sword, toes, feet and legs disappeared into the watery depths and the beam of light slowly faded. The curtain of mist then re-descended while could be heard the sound of flapping wings as a flight of wild geese left the mystical scene.

Bemused by the wondrous spectacle Bedivere eventually returned to the hollow where Arthur lay now a mere shadow of his former regal self. His skin was ashen and his breath weak. The reaper of souls was indeed at his shoulder.

Arthur beckoned Bedivere closer. “I heard the celestial chorus” he said quietly “but what did you see my dear friend, what did you see?” So, the old knight Bedivere told of what he saw when he took up Excalibur and cast it away. He told him of seeing the mist lifting. The sword suspended in the beam of light and the upheld female legs, as if in a ballet, moving in circles first this way then that through the water. There the good Bedivere halted in his account for fear that further telling of his wondrous tale would not be believed. “And?” breathless, the King questioned through congealed blood-stained lips “And what else did you see?” Bedivere hesitated then said. “I saw all the ladies' feet come together around the hilt of the sword and then feet, legs and the sword Excalibur disappeared beneath the ripples of the water and as the music came to an end the light faded and the mist once more returned and shrouded the lake.

“You have done well” said Arthur. “Now I can die in peace in the knowledge the over fifties, Avalon ladies synchronised swimming club, of which I am patron, is still thriving. Is still going strong. I pray it will do so long after I have gone.”

With that said, Arthur Pendragon, King of all Britain (including Basildon) took his last breath, closed his eyes and died.

Loosely based on Thomas Malory's Morte d'Arthur 15th Cent

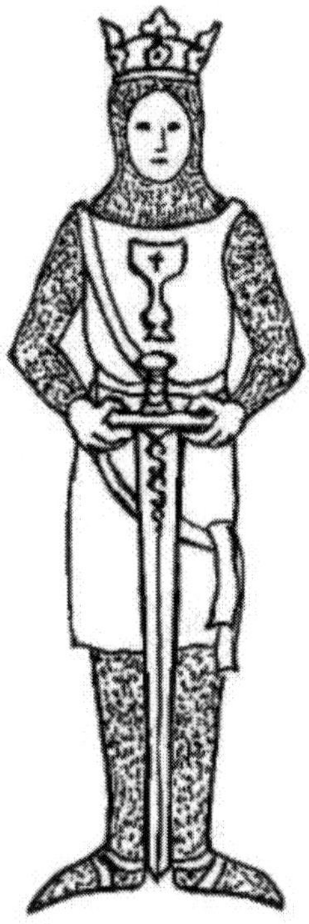

The Fisherman's Boy

Below high ragged cliffs where on sunny days the iridescent salt sea water is a translucent turquoise there lies a cove in which nestles a small village of close-knit fishing folk.

Many years ago, among that hard-working community lived a single father and son who were devoted to each other. Sadly, the boy never knew his mother for she died soon after bringing him into the world. As had been her dying wish, she was buried at sea so that she would be among the grey seals that basked and swam off that rocky Cornish coast. Those seals she felt such fondness for.

Since she and the boy's father first met by the water's edge on a moonlit night there had been a cured and tanned grey seal skin hanging on thc wall of the cottage, which her husband lovingly placed over her in her coffin the day she passed away; after which all that then remained of her in the homely cottage was a loving memory and a lighter area on the stone wall where the pelt had hung.

From a very early age the boy would often ask about his mother, and his fisherman father would tell of how beautiful and kind she was with a freshness about her like the salt sea spray; and how when she sung her voice calmed the wind and stilled the waves. But he never spoke of nor explained the lighter patch on the wall, even though his son would often inquire. However, not understanding how or why, the fisherman's boy (that being the name by which he became known) soon found that by gently touching and caressing the light grey area, which was warmer than the rest of the wall, he could experience a feeling of comfort and love. A kind of comfort and love only a mother could give.

That's not to say that his father lacked affection for his son (for that was certainly not the case) but being a hard-working fisherman with a living to make to support both himself and the boy he wasn't able to give his son all the attention he wished to, or the kind of love his son craved.

However, the boy's father was a great storyteller and if he hadn't become a fisherman like his father and his father before him, he would have become a Drool-Teller travelling from village to village, town to town, across the width and breath of his native Cornwall. Such an ambition was never fulfilled but on the dark evenings when his boat was idle and moored in the safety of the small harbour he would sit with his son and tell him stories of the sea.

Stories of pirates, of smugglers, and the wreckers with their misleading lantern lights as they galloped backwards and forwards across the high cliff tops on dark steeds, with muffled hooves and bridle bits, to confuse seafarers so that unwittingly they might bring their vessels near to the jagged rocks off that coast; where their ships bound for Falmouth and such ports would smash and spill their cargo to be salvaged from the waves by anonymous country 'Gentlemen' who profitably exploited a stormy moonless night.

Many such tales he spun in that candle-lit cottage. Tales about armed Excise men hiding behind creaking stable doors or behind ivy-clad tombstones in the local churchyard waiting to pounce and recover contraband of rum, tobacco, fine silk, and French woven lace. And then there were the stories of the strange creatures that inhabited the surrounding moors and the yarns concerning Piskies, and the tricks they play-although they sometimes have a wicked sense of humour, they will do good and help anyone who treat them with respect.

And as if to follow their example, within his tales the boy's father always included a moral or two, as a way to illustrate good kind-hearted conduct and at all times he ended such a story with the phrase "Those that are good will reap reward for what goes around, comes round!"

While his father was about his business upon the ocean the fisherman's boy would, at low tide, wander along the sea shore looking into the wondrously colourful underwater world of the rock pools. When he found small fish floundering in the shallows, left behind by an outgoing tide, he would scoop them up in his shrimping net and take them out to where the waves lapped across the golden sands. There he would throw them back in the ocean singing.

Throw them back in the ocean
Throw them back from the shore
Throw them back to the salty sea
So they may live some more.

When the fisherman's boy grew older, at high tide he would go down to the small harbour with his father from where they would take the family fishing boat out upon the water. There he would help to cast the nets and when eventually they hauled them back in over the gunnels and on to the deck the fisherman's boy would sort the catch by type and size. But the smaller fish he would always throw back while happily singing.

Throw them back to the ocean
As we sail back to the shore
Throw them back to the ocean
So they may live some more.

He loved his life on the water. The smell of the sea. The wind in his hair. Also, he loved to watch the seals basking on the rocks and enjoyed the company of one in particular that would dive in and swim around and under the boat with her pups then softly grunting would bob up and down in the water with them while all the time seemingly watching him as well. He often envied those young seals having a mother to take care of them and giving the kind of love and understanding only a mother could give.

As autumn follows summer, eventually the father died leaving the cottage and the boat to his son, now a grown man. It wasn't long after that sad day, when the fisherman's boy (for that was still the name by which he was known there about) was preparing to set sail on that evening's ebb tide, that elderly Miss Dorothy Procter, the local postmistress, arrived on the quay advising that due to a weather warning about an approaching storm she had heard broadcast on the her wireless he shouldn't set sail.

"Thank you. I am grateful for your advice" said the fisherman's boy "but I have to earn a living. My father and I weathered many a storm." "But this one" Dorothy protested "is said to be more severe than we will have seen on our shores for many a year. By all accounts there's a mighty south westerly building up in the Bay of Biscay that will be coming across the Atlantic towards us." "I wouldn't believe everything you hear on that 'wireless' of yours if I were you. Weathermen are known to get things wrong" said the fisherman's boy wryly.

While they were chatting, other villagers concerned for the fisherman's boy's safety made their way down to the harbour. "Don't you worry about me" he said to the assembled crowd. "If there is going to be a so-called storm and it hasn't already petered out by the time it reaches our coast, I will be home and dry sitting on the strand downing a good pint of Scrumpy. Anyway, I have my sou'wester with me" he said jokingly as he put it on at a funny angle in an attempt to make them laugh. But no one did. "Listen" he said, "I will be alright. I promise you. The weather man has got it wrong." "Don't go, don't go" he heard them shouting as he left the quay.

So the Fisherman's boy sailed into the west
Out into the west as the sun went down
For to bring fish home he would do his best.
Then rest awhile upon the strand
Then rest awhile upon the strand.

For men must work and women weep
There's little to earn, out there on the deep, if
The harbour bar be moaning, if
The harbour bar be moaning.

The Harbour master in the light house tower
Trimmed his lamp as the sun went down
He looked at the squall and he looked at the shower, as
The small boat passed below him, as
The small boat passed below him.

For men must work and women weep
Though storms be sudden and the water deep, and
The harbour bar be moaning, and
The harbour bar be moaning.

And indeed, it was moaning, in a most fearful sorrowful way. For a brief moment the fisherman's boy had second thoughts about venturing out on the ebb tide for he remembered well the legend his father used to tell about the sound of a tide going out over the harbour sand bar. “If it should make a moaning sound” he used to say; “then that was a warning of an impending disaster.” (Which you my intrepid reader I am sure have already envisaged might be the case.)

But as quickly as that thought had come there came another to take its place. That men must work.

Soon his boat was clear of the harbour and its sand bar heading far out into deeper water. Out there alone, while the fisherman's boy prepared to cast his nets in readiness to chase the mackerel, the squall rapidly changed into something more sinister; a force 9 gale, bearing down on him and creating gigantic waves. The mighty storm had arrived to wreak havoc and devastation. The boat was quickly awash with cold Atlantic water and rapidly started to sink below the waves taking the fisherman's boy with it towards a watery grave.

With an innate instinct for survival he broke free from the water-logged timbers of the boat and desperately struggled to stay afloat, to ride the waves and keep his head above water but as his strength diminished, he knew it to be in vain as he silently sunk below the waves of the cruel unrepentant sea.

By the next morning the storm had abated and veered off down the English Channel leaving the tiny fishing village virtually unscathed. And as the sun was rising the villagers, having first called in at the fisherman's boy's cottage and finding nobody at home, made their way down to the shore in the forlorn hope that the fisherman's boy might have outrun the storm and survived the night. A search amidst the other craft within and along the outer wall of the small harbour gave no results other than a sickly feeling in many a stomach that he, that many had known since a baby, was now lost to them forever. Franticly they scanned the strand but all they could see were clumps of seaweed and a few seals near the rocks below the cliffs. at the far end of the sandy beach.

Then came a shout from the Harbour Master high in the lighthouse tower. "Over there" he yelled pointing towards the outcrop of rocks. "No" someone else shouted back "It's only the seals."

"Yes" yelled back the Harbour Master holding his telescope to his eye. "But there is a body among them partially covered in what looks like a seal skin. I'm sure it's the fisherman's boy."

There lay a body on the shining sand
In the morning light, as the tide went down
The villagers wept, wringing their hands
For the fisherman's boy lying there on the strand
For the fisherman's boy lying there on the strand.

For men must work and women weep
There's nothing to earn, out there on the deep, when
The harbour bar is moaning, when
The harbour bar is moaning.

As the villagers approached, the small colony of seals wriggled and flipper-clawed their way down the beach then slid into the tide and swam from view round the headland leaving just one bobbing about in the waves and softly grunting as it watched the villagers gathering around the body of the fisherman's boy lying there motionless under the cover of a grey seal pelt.

It was Old Peter Hearn, a local storyteller and collector of tales, who stepped forward and cautiously lifted the seal skin. As he did so the fisherman's boy moved, then started to get up. Startled, the crowd stepped back a pace or two as, swaying a little, he rose to his feet. Soon he was standing upright before them as alive and well as any of those witnessing the extraordinary happening.

In the midst of great excitement and jubilation, that included many questions, eventually there was a moment of silence in which the fisherman's boy was able to relate what he could remember of his safe deliverance from the storm.

"I had given up." he said "I had no strength left to stay afloat. To stay alive. It was then as I started to lose consciousness and began to sink, I felt a nudging and tickling of many small fish lifting me back up to the surface to breathe. There I heard a beautiful voice of comfort that calmed the wind and stilled the waves as she sang

Save him from the ocean
Take him back to the shore.
Save him from the salty sea
So he can live some more.

"Don't you see" he continued "It was the little fishes that saved me. It was them that kept me afloat and brought me back to this shore and safely home. "But what about the seal skin?" someone asked, "how did you come by that to cover you and keep you warm while you lay here?" "I don't know" replied the fisherman's boy. "That bit is all a blur, a complete mystery, but I will take it home with me. I have just the place for it to always remind me that comfort can come in the strangest of ways from the strangest of places."

And to conclude this story that's what he did. He took the grey seal pelt home and hung it on the wall and found it fitted exactly edge to edge over the lighter patch of the stone and there I believe it remains to this very day.

"But didn't he cure the skin first?" I hear you ask. The answer to that question is No, because the strangest thing of all is… it had already been well treated and was as soft and cuddlesome as a mother is to her child.

My basic inspiration for this story comes from a story I heard told by oral storyteller, author and friend Peter Hearn at, I believe, the 1999 Chippenham Folk Festival. My reference to the 'harbour bar moaning' comes from a verse in the poem/ballad Three Fishers by Charles Kingsley 1851. *There is an old legend from the fishing towns of western England. that if the withdrawing tide made a moaning sound over the bar, that was a portent of disaster, betokening the coming death of those who cross it. The "bar" is a sand bar across the entrance to a small harbour. that keeps the water comparatively still and calm within the harbour itself.*

A Wish Too Far

Upon a scraggy piece of land on an island off the shore of East Essex stood a small tatty rumbled tumbled down cottage in which there lived a mild-mannered man who had a nagging wife. Nag, nag, nag she did from morning till night and even then, when the poor man should have had some respite, she was known to nag him in her sleep. Nag nag nag. She never stopped. Sometimes with good reason but mostly without she would Nag, nag, nag.

It's fair to say her husband did little around the cottage, as I have already mentioned in similar words, it was very much run down, and needed a lot of love and care but all enthusiasm once shown by the husband to keep the property in good shape had long since passed, due to the never ceasing nagging. Even when he banged in a nail his wife would nag him to extract it again to prove he had knocked it in straight. And on its removal, it would inevitably bend which then set the woman off again nagging that he hadn't hammered it in straight and true in the first place and he should replace it with a new nail. And so it was, with every job she would nag nag nag him so much so that nothing ever really got finished. In the end he gave up starting such projects and just allowed himself to be subject to her incessant nagging.

However, there was one place he was able to find solace from the relentless verbal ear- bashing from his wife with her nag, nag nagging and that was in the solitude of fishing out on the water of the vast cold North Sea. He was even more than happy for her to nag for him to go. Normally he didn't fish too far out from the shore but just far enough to be out of hearing of her constant nagging, and although at times he could see her pacing up and down the shore and mouthing words in his direction all he could hear was the sound of the wind, the waves and the cry of the sea birds.

One day something urged him to row further out and cast his baited hook into deeper water and from out there he found it quite satisfying at not even being able to see his wife and feel completely free of her. It wasn't long before there was a movement and then a definite tugging on the line. The man decided to let his catch run with the bait for a while, but it did nothing of the kind and of its own accord swam towards him, then leapt high from the water and landed with a big wet fish sounding flop at his feet in the bottom of the boat. Instantly the man reached for the priest- not of the holy kind but a wooden club to dispatch his quarry with. However just as he was going to strike the defenceless creature it looked up at him and said "Hello it's your lucky day. This is 'Take a risk, kiss a fish and make a wish week'. I'm a fish of a magical kind. If you take me off your hook, give me a kiss then throw me back letting me live I will grant you a wish."

For a moment the man just sat there in sheer amazement, not believing what he had just seen and heard. A talking fish. How was that possible. The whole situation was very unnerving to the mild-mannered man. The fish sensed its captor's predicament and said "I tell you what. As a special offer, if you want, you can cut out the 'kissy' bit. Just remove the hook and throw me back and you can still make a wish." "Well in that case, no offence meant, if you don't mind, I will just remove the hook and release you back into the water and I'm sorry if I've caused you any pain" replied the man. "That's very thoughtful of you to consider that I might be suffering some pain with a barbed hook through the upper part of my mouth" said the fish "but moving on; what's your wish?" "My wish" said the man thoughtfully "is that my rundown home becomes a lovely well maintained newly thatched, white painted cottage with lattice windows and sweet-smelling pink roses round the door then perhaps my wife might stop nagging me. Yes that is my wish." "It will be done" said the fish although I can't promise the last bit. Once a nagger always a nagger. They are very seldom satisfied."

With the hook carefully removed the fish was released back into the sea and sure enough when the man returned to shore there, instead of the small rumbled tumbled down cottage stood a beautiful newly thatched, white painted one with lattice windows and sweet-smelling pink roses round the front door. "Look husband" said his wife "look at our home. I went to market and when I returned this is what I found. Did you get the builders in? How was it done so quickly?"

"I caught a fish, a magic fish who granted me a wish" said the husband sheepishly. "Magic fish" said his wife excitedly. Where is it? I'll run the bath. We will keep it in there. I will tell it to straight away change the colour of the roses round the door. I want red roses not pink. I hate pink." And she nagged and nagged. Oh my goodness did she nag!

"I let it go. I released it, put it back in the sea" said the man. "You did what?" exclaimed his wife. "Why do that?" "That was part of the deal" her husband replied. "If I let it go it would grant me a wish which it has as you can see before you. A beautiful new well-maintained cottage." "You foolish husband" screamed his wife. "I want a large house not this silly little cottage. I want a huge Mansion with a long tree lined avenue leading up to an impressive ornate front door. You must go out first thing tomorrow and catch that fish again and don't bother returning until you do" "I will never be able to catch that same fish again" replied her husband. "Don't you realise how vast and deep the North Sea is?" But his wife refused to listen. All she did was nag and nag and even continued nagging in her sleep.

The next morning the husband rowed out across the water more to get away from the nag, nag nagging than in the belief that he would ever catch the very same fish again. However, the seeming impossible happened. His hook and line had only been in the water for three minutes when there was a tugging at its end followed by the fish leaping into the boat and looking up and saying "Hello it's your lucky day. This is 'Take a risk, kiss a fish and make a wish week.' I'm a fish of the magical kind. If you… Oh it's you again! Didn't you're wish come true then?" "Indeed it did" replied the man "but my wife wasn't satisfied with what I wished for. She wanted more. Something bigger" "Some do" said the fish sympathetically. "Nag, nag nagged you to come back out here to catch me again did she?" "Yes" said the man hanging his head somewhat shamefully.

"Well" said the fish "we had better get on with it. I suppose the kiss is still out of the question?" "Yes if you don't mind" said the other apologetically as he carefully removed the hook "After all I am married man." Both he and the fish laughed.

Yes, my faithful reader, it's hard to believe a fish being able to laugh. A magical fish who can grant wishes is quite plausible in fact utterly without question believable as well we know but a fish able to laugh! However, it's part of this story as told to me therefore I'm inclined to let this absurdity remain.

"So, what's the wish to be this time" inquired the magical fish. (Which was also able to laugh.) "In place of the cottage the wife has nagged me for a huge Mansion with a long tree lined avenue leading up to an impressive ornate front door" requested the man embarrassedly. "Very well" said the fish. "Put me back in the water and your wish shall be granted."

And it was. When the man arrived back at the shore and moored his boat, he then took a long walk down a tree lined avenue to a huge mansion with an impressive ornate front door where stood his wife. "Happy now?" he hesitantly enquired. "This place is far too small" complained his wife. I want a palace" she demanded. But" said her husband. "No buts" she screamed "You get in that silly little boat of yours, catch that clever fish again and tell it you want a palace with a hundred rooms, marble floors, solid gold chandeliers, servants and everything and all besides. Yes, tell it to furnish it with everything the greatest of palaces have and more." demanded his nagging wife. "But" interjected her husband. "I said no buts" quickly retorted the woman. "And also" she continued. "Tell that slippery scaly friend of yours to make us King and Queen with robes of the finest silk trimmed with ermine. And before you say anything about using real fur. Don't."

Then after a brief moments' thought she said "Forget the King'y and Queen'y bit. Tell it. No, DEMAND IT to turn us into Gods." "Gods!" exclaimed the husband! "Don't you think that's going a bit too far?" "GODS, GODS, you a God and me a GODDESS" she screamed at him as she turned her back and walked into the mansion.

Shaking his head in utter disbelief at his wife's wild request he took the long walk down the tree lined avenue back to his boat and rowed far out from the shore. After casting out his fishing line it wasn't long before there in the bottom of the boat was the now familiar magic fish looking up and saying "Hello it's your lucky day. This is 'Take a risk, kiss a fish and make a wish week.' I'm a fish of a magical kind. If you take me off your hook…" Then stopping in mid patter said "Oh no not you again. We have got to stop meeting like this. I take it your wife is still not satisfied and has been nag, nag nagging you again for something bigger. So, what is it to be this time?" The man, while gently removing the hook, red faced with embarrassment, reluctantly told the fish that his wife wished to live in a Palace and not only that, but she had demanded that she become a Goddess and he a God." The fish said nothing, not a single word and with eyes glazed over it now just lay there seemingly lifeless in the bottom of the boat. The man confused and not wishing the fish to die picked it up and carefully, lovingly placed it back into the sea to stimulate a revival. There it lay motionless on its side on the water's surface then all of a sudden it flicked its tail and disappeared into the depths below the waves.

The man slowly rowed back to the shore to where his wife was frantically running around and around what he recognised to be the old small tatty rumbled tumbled down cottage screaming "What have you done? I'm still a mortal. I asked that we be GODS. Where is the Palace I told you to wish for, and where's the Mansion gone with its long tree lined avenue leading up to its impressive ornate front door? Also, where is the beautiful newly thatched, white painted cottage? Where's that? The one with the lattice windows and the wrong colour sweet smelling roses round the front door. Where has that gone? What have you done husband, what have you done?" And she nagged and nagged and nagged some more until at last she took a breath and in that pause for air her husband was able to reply. "It's not what I have done. It's what you have done. As a result of your continuous nagging and never being satisfied with what you have and always wishing for something more you went one wish too far. Now you have nothing but what we started with" said the husband. "You get back in that boat this instant and go out there and catch that fish and bring it back here" commanded his wife and she nagged and nagged and nagged some more.

For three days and three nights the husband sat in his boat fishing until at last there was a tug on his line and then in no time at all there at his feet was the fish saying, "Hello it's your lucky day this is 'Take a risk, kiss a fish and make a wish week' extended by popular demand. I'm a fish of a magical kind. If you take me off your hook, give me a kiss then throw me back and let me live I will grant you a wish."

So pleased was the husband of the nagging wife that in his joy of once more catching the same fish he straight away removed the hook and picking up the fish squeezed his eyes shut and gave it a big kiss. When at last he again opened his eyes, looking down he found that he himself now had a fish's tail and was holding in his arms a most beautiful mermaid.

"I thought you were a married man" she said with a laugh. "I am" he said "but I can't stand the wife's constant nag, nag nagging any longer. She truly has a heart of stone so much so I wish she be turned into that hard substance. She is now no more to me than an insignificant pebble on a beach."

The mermaid smiled, then gently taking him by the hand together they slid into the water and dived deep below the waves and although they were never ever seen again I the teller of this tale I'm convinced, as I write here upon this page; they lived happily ever after.

And what of his nagging wife? Well, somewhere on the shore of a scraggy piece of land on an island off the Essex coast, if you are so inclined to look, you just might find a pebble in the sand with a hole through it. If you do, that is her. The hole being her mouth wide open as if nagging. Nag nag nagging forever nagging.

And if you my reader of this tale are a woman then wear that stone on a string around your neck as a reminder not to nag. And if you the finder are a man, then dig deeply in the sand and bury that stone as quickly as you can.

Many years ago, I believe, I first heard a version of this tale told by renowned Storyteller and friend Taffy Thomas MBE at a performance in Cecil Sharpe House home of The English Folk Dance and Song Society.

Taffy was awarded his MBE in 2001 for his services to Storytelling. He also became Laureate for Storytelling.2010-2012.

The Oak and the Blade

A slant on an Aesop fable

Once upon a time, there stood an Oak. All the vegetation around him thought him handsome and strong (which indeed he was) but more importantly, due to his age, he had wisdom granted to him by the Creator.

One day, as dark clouds tumbled across the sky in a desperate race to swallow the sun, a young slim, blade of grass looked up and said. “Oak tree, you appear very strong and able to stand your ground but, if a mighty gale were to come then I'm sure you would eventually be blown down. Whereas I, a blade of grass would not. For I am able to bend and sway in the strongest of winds.”

“Oh yes” said the Oak, “that is indeed true. But if, as you say I was blown down then my fruit the acorn will spill, and in time spring up and become a mighty tree like me who all will come to admire. Whereas you, small blade of grass, who prefers to keep sweet, but cuts like a knife, bends with the wind then shivers at the slightest breeze; you will always be trodden under foot.”

The Man in the Green Suit

Tick tock, tick tock went the clock. Tick tock, tick tock. At last the man in the green suit realized he had a story to tell and so excited was he to tell someone, he immediately rushed out into the street from the George Hotel and told his story to the first person he met.

Now, it so happens that person was a collector of stories, a storyteller. “That's a fine story” said the storyteller. “Might I tell it?” “Of course you can, I have no use of it now” said the man in the green suit.

The storyteller thanked the man in the green suit and the next day while telling his stories to a small crowd sitting under an old oak tree on the village green overlooking the River Tees, he included the story that had been kindly given to him by the man in thc green suit.

In this small, but spell bound crowd, there was also two other people who collected and told stories. “We loved all your stories” they said as the storyteller was packing up ready to leave. “But most of all we liked the story that you said was given to you by the man in the green suit. That was our favourite. Do you mind if we told that story?” “Not at all” said the storyteller brushing some grass clippings off his trousers and removing an oak leaf from his hair which had left its branch at a most convenient time whilst he had been telling, from his vast repertoire, his Oak and the Blade story. “I'm sure that it would please the man in the green suit to know that his story is being shared. That’s what stories are for. To share are they not?” “Indeed they are” was their enthusiastic reply.

The next day there were now three storytellers in three different parts of the county telling the story first told by the man in the green suit and unbelievable as it might seem to most people (although I'm sure it's not so for such an ardent reader of my stories as your good self) but in each separate crowd there were four people who were also collectors and tellers of stories. And the next day, well, I'm sure you've guessed!

And so, it went on and on with more and more people hearing and telling the story first told by the man in the green suit. Until, many, many years later it appeared that everyone in County Durham and beyond knew the story, first told... by the man in the green suit.

But that is, as it turned out, all except the man in the green suit. For as I have said, it was many years later and as some of us know only too well, as the years pass our memories can tend to fade. And this was very true in the case of the man in the green suit. And on hearing the story, and not remembering that it was he who had first told it, so excited he was to tell someone, sadly his heart gave out and in that instant the clock... stopped ticking.

In 1875, an American songwriter named Henry Work stayed at the George Hotel in the village of Piercebridge, County Durham. In the reception area there was a large pendulum clock. The clock was said to have stopped dead on the day the last owner died. That story inspired him to pen the poem/song 'Grandfather's Clock' When years ago I first wrote my story 'The Man in the Green Suit' in its original form I knew nothing of the story associated with 'Grandfather's Clock.' It was only when I decided in my tale to change 'old gilded mantelpiece clock' for another type of clock I came upon the story of the origins of the name Grandfather Clock. So, by changing a few words here and there I have now given my story a location which it didn't have before. I hope you my reader enjoyed it.

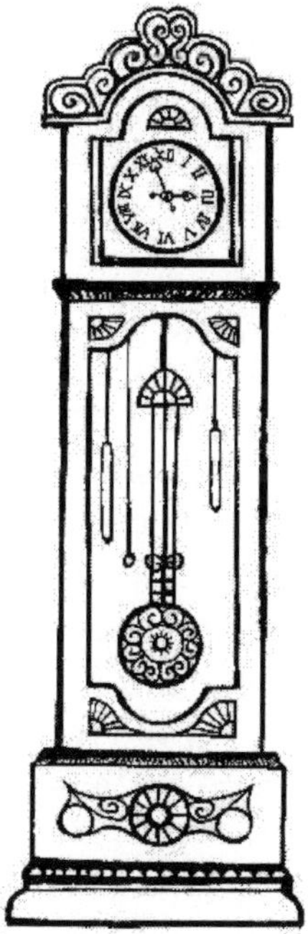

Arthur and the Butterfly

So many stories abound of Arthur as a man, as a King, and of his heroic deeds and those of his Knights of the Round Table. But just like there are very few stories about the early years of Jesus; stories of Arthur as a child and as a teenager are equally scarce. However, here upon this page I hope, in some small way, to rectify this with the story I now relate.

This story, as you would expect, happened, as many good stories do, a very, very long time ago in a land of legend and misty dreams. That land was the mystical island of Avalon. The Apple Isle. The Isle of plenty where man didn't have to toil on the land. Nature herself provided in abundance all that was required.

This was the Isle where the four winds met, new born stars gathered their energy and old stars went to die. The very same place where the wizard Merlin brought up Arthur the newborn bastard son of King Uther Pendragon.

You who are reading these words might well remember from other accounts, in other books, that it was the lustful Uther that begged the magician Merlin to transform him into the semblance of Gorlois Duke of Cornwall so that he could trick, deceive, rape and impregnate with his royal seed, Ingraine the young Duke's loyal wife. In return for such powerful wizardry Uther agreed to the enchanter's condition that the first boy born of that union would be Merlin's to take and bring up as his own until the appointed time he would inherit his father's crown.

And so, it was on a winter's night when the snow lay heavy on the ground Merlin transformed himself into an

Eagle Owl and with the stars and moon to guide his way, he flew to Tintagel to collect the royal child.

While Ingraine slept soundly beside the cradle in which lay her first-born Arthur, lovingly wrapped in a warm soft fleece, Merlin entered the open casement and silently swooped and gently snatched up the child in his talons and in an instant was gone; out into the cold night air.

Looking after and bringing up a child was not as easy as Merlin might first have thought. Some say that doing so aged him terribly and turned his head hair and beard completely white. First there were the sleepless nights. Then the tearful screaming ab dab's and tantrums of "I want this, I want that" and "it's not fair." Followed by the "Are we there yet" and the "I'm bored" stage in the growing up process with yet more to come... The dreaded teenage years.

Merlin was not only father he was also mentor and ran a school in a shady grove at the north end of the mystical island for his young charge and only pupil Arthur. There he taught the boy such things as Astronomy, astrology, and chemistry (known back then as alchemy.) He was also particularly insistent that Arthur should master all the languages and dialects of Britain and at the same time, somewhat reluctantly, a little bit of French.

It was while teaching the honourable subjects of humility and compassion that he tried most of all to instil in Arthur attributes of wisdom (which to be truthful often fell on deaf ears as it does with most boys in their teens.)

I think it fair to say that as a teenager Arthur was a cocky so and so. Such an opinion I believe you my reader might well share when you have read a little further.

It was on one fine summer's morning when Arthur was making his way to school across the strikingly colourful meadows of wild flowers that he spotted a butterfly. He sat for a while watching it feeding on the nectar and a thought came to him that maybe Merlin wasn't as clever and as wise as everyone believed him to be and gave him credit for.

Following that train of thought Arthur stealthily moved towards the butterfly and reaching forward gently encased the fragile fluttering insect between his youthful cupped hands. Then looking through his fingers at his captive he said “What I will do is take you, my beautiful winged creature, concealed in my hands to Merlin and I shall say to him. Merlin if you be so clever and wise tell me, what is it I gently hold hidden in my hands? And if he should answer correctly 'A Butterfly'. (which there is a good chance he will; remembering I brought one of your kind in such a way to show him when I was merely a fascinated young innocent child) then I will say to him yes but tell me is this one dead or is it alive? And if he should say 'Alive' then I will bring my hands together in a vice like grip to crush and squeeze the very life out of you then open up my hands and show him your dust like remains. But if he should answer 'Dead' then, my little delicate creature it will be your lucky day for I will open up my hands giving you back your freedom to fly away and become again at one with nature.”

With his plan firmly set he continued his journey towards the grove where Merlin held his school in a cave carved into the side of grassy hill on top of which grew a thorn tree.

Upon Arthur's casual arrival Merlin stepped out into the glade and looking up at the sun he said “Late again. I don't know. You teenagers, up half the night doing whatever you do then can't get up in the mornings. Now when I was a boy...” “And when was that exactly old man?” interrupted Arthur sarcastically. “Oh way before the mists of time” replied Merlin but I'm not too old to give you a clip round the ear for your impertinence. Now be wise, sit down Arthur and let's get on.” “On the subject of being wise” confidently replied the youngster “If you yourself be wise, as wise as people say you are. Tell me Merlin what have I here, cupped in my hands?” “You are trying my patience boy” retorted the Wizard. “It's a butterfly. Now let’s proceed with your schooling.”

“It is indeed a butterfly, that I think would be quite obvious to a jack ass perched upside down on a bean pole but tell me” said Arthur “is this butterfly dead or alive.”

Merlin fixed the youth with a hard-cold stare and said “It's in your hands Arthur. In your hands.” ... And somewhere an owl hooted.

If my memory serves me correctly, I had just climbed up the snake path to the summit of Mazda when I first heard the like of this story as a Buddhist story concerning the Dalai Lama and one of his Tibetan students.

The Student and the Angler

"What you doing then" enquired the youth leaning up against the pleasure pier's walkway safety rail as he loudly licked his recently purchased Rossi ice-cream. "Excuse me" said the lone man within earshot "Were you talking to me?" "Yep", replied the young man as he now munched on the chocolate wafer flake stuck in the cold cream.

A pier train rattled past taking a happy throng of day-trippers back a mile and a bit to the shore. "Sorry what did you say?" said the man. "Yep. I said Yep" replied the youth.

"Yep what" questioned the man trying to raise his voice above a passing group of mildly tipsy middle-aged revellers in Kiss-me-Quick hats on their way to that particular year's end of the pier Thursday afternoon variety show Zip-A-Hoy at the sun deck Theatre; "I was talking to you asking what you were doing. Just trying to be friendly that's all I'm a student at the College" said the youth.

"I'm fishing" said the man as he gazed over the edge into the tidal waters of the Thames. "Why what did you think I was doing, darning socks?" he said a little annoyed.

"I see you only have one rod" replied the student. "Now if you were to have two rods you would catch twice as many fish"

"And then what" interjected the man as he reeled in a little of the fishing line

"Then you would have more fish to sell and eventually with the money you would be able to buy many more rods and catch many more fish with which to trade" exclaimed the young proposer.

Another train noisily clattered by on its return journey towards the crowded pier head after which the man replied, “Then what do you propose I do?”

“Well” said the student feeling quite in charge of the dialogue between the two. “With the profit you could buy a boat and catch more fish”

“Then what” said the angler a little tired of the conversation as he slowly reeled in a little more line and a seagull perched expectantly on the handrail next to him.

“Then” continued the youth “With the profit you would be able to purchase a fleet of boats and employ others to fish for you.”

From somewhere Radio Caroline could be heard blurring out from a transistor radio. “And then what” asked the man reeling in the remainder of the line to reveal nothing on the end but the hook while the gull left its perch and took flight towards another angler further along the pier walkway.

“Well”, said the student pleased to be passing on some of the knowledge he had obtained from the book on Economics by Colin R Freshman he had recently purchased from Bobin's Bookshop ready for his return to the college after the summer break.

“Then you could open up a fish processing factory and employ hundreds of people and become very rich indeed...”

Swift, the red motor speedboat roared past on the water below accompanied by screams of happiness from its occupants, a group of young female day trippers.

“And then” said the angler packing his fishing equipment away. “What then?”

“Well then” said the student with a big grin on his face “you will be able to retire and take up a nice peaceful hobby like sea fishing.”

"And that's just what I've recently done. Retired; but taking up sea fishing just as a peaceful hobby it would seem is now a little harder these days. Good afternoon to you and keep up the reading" said the angler as he strolled off to walk the mile and a bit back down the pier towards the shore where was parked his limousine. On his arrival the chauffeur held open the car door and tipping his peaked cap said, "Where to Mr Freshman?"

I have been telling the essence of this story for years but for the purpose of this book I decided to view it in a different way and set it on the 'The Longest Pleasure Pier in the World'.

Zip-A-Hoy was a popular end of the pier show of the early 60s. Produced by Jerry Jerome. It often starred his partner and choreographer Roberta Pett.

Jerry also produced pantomimes which also had Roberta in leading roles.

They lived in Rochford, Essex and owned a Theatrical Warehouse in the High Street Shoeburyness.

Radio Caroline (a Pirate radio station) operated some miles off shore from Felixstowe.

Bobins bookshop was situated in the Victoria (Talza) Arcade. Demolished in the late Sixties

The Cutlass Stone

As Jack walked down old Leigh Street
A press gang there he chanced to meet
They demanded he should join the fleet
On board a man-o-war, boys
On board a man-o-war.

Possibly a strange introduction to a story but please bear with me dear reader and all will be revealed.

It was early one Sunday morning while many of the inhabitants of the sleepy fishing village were indeed still fast asleep. That is except for those who like young Jack and his family were Church goers and therefore up bright and early to administer to various morning chores like raking out the ashes from the previous night's wood fire in preparation to re-lay and kindle new warmth for a late afternoon winter's nap.

With a new dawn now breaking bringing with it the sun to adorn a cloudless sky all was well with the world; or so it seemed. For unbeknown to Jack, or the rest of the drowsy community, under the cover of the early morning misty darkness came a Press Gang rowing silently upon the incoming tide. So skilled where those matelots of the British Navy that their rag muffled oars made no sound, splash or ripple as they stealthily brought their gig alongside the wharf.

"Time we were going." shouted Jack to Molly his wife, who was upstairs in the small one bedroom weather boarded fisherman cottage getting the three children dressed and ready for church. "They need feeding first."

Molly yelled back while trying to find a missing shoe which she believed was somewhere under the inadequately sized bed in which all the family, other than baby Timothy, slept head to toe. Newly born Tim slept in a drawer on the floor. "We haven't really got the time. We are already late. They will have to have some biscuits on the way" said Jack. "Found it" shouted his wife, "Found what?" Jack shouted back "The shoe" Molly joyfully replied. "It was in the drawer with the baby."

Eventually, all dressed in their Sunday best and to the sound of the last pull of the bells calling all to prayer, they started to make their way towards Horse Hill (Leigh Hill as some now prefer to call it) when out from a passageway off Alley Dock stepped a burly seaman and behind him seven more. "Wants to join the Navy do you? he questioned in an oafish manner while obstructing Jack and his family from any further progress along the street. "I thank you for asking Sir, but I have no desire to join the Navy. Now if you don't mind, we will be on our way" replied Jack. "We would normally get some 'gangers' to do this work for us continued the unruly sailor but you landlubbers 'ere about are too knit a community." Then spitting on the ground, he barked "Grab 'im lads" "I said no thank you. I have no wish to join Sir" replied Jack as another of the marauding gang grasped hold of Jack's arm dragging him away from his wife and children. "You leave my Jack be" shrieked Molly as she, with fists flying, set about her husband's assailant. That was until she was held from behind by two others of the Press Gang one of which, while being constantly kicked in the shins by Jack's three young children, put his hand over Molly's mouth in an attempt to stop her screaming. But it was to no avail as the sailor was soon to find out when Molly, determined to remove his grubby smelly fingers from her ruby lips, sunk her teeth deep into the podgy flesh and as he shouted out with pain and released his grip Molly shouted louder at the top of her voice “Run Jack run. Up to the church they won't go in there.”

Jack broke free and ran away
up to Saint Clements for to pray
not to sail on any day
On board a man-o-war, boys
On board a man-o-war.

Along the crudely cobbled street windows opened and bleary-eyed villagers popped their heads out to see what all the commotion was about. The gang were by then in pursuit of their quarry but were no match for Jack's nimbleness. Too much time at sea and too much rum in the belly had made them sluggish on land in comparison with Jack's speed and agility.

By the time Jack reached and entered God's house through the red bricked porch (a Tudor addition to the earlier 15th century structure) the sung Angelus was at its end. Jack piously crossed himself with holy water from the stoup then quietly whispered to the Verger who then whispered just as quietly to the Rector.

Upon their arrival at the church the press gang made to enter but found their way physically barred by the Rector who refused to have swords or any other weapons inside the ancient Kentish rag stone church and said in a stern voice “Here we live by the cross and not by the sword.” then in a softer tone continued “However if you would all like to leave your cutlasses, knives, clubs and whatever out here then gentlemen you are most welcome to sing, kneel and pray with us gentler folk. I am fully aware your business is authorized by parliament but remember a church is a place of sanctuary and it is morally wrong and unholy to remove anyone from within by force.”

Those roughneck sailors knew only too well that it was a punishable offence to leave their weapons unattended in case they got stolen and also, they thought they knew the law regarding sanctuary which they believed would forbid them to snatch Jack or any other man or boy from inside the church so therefore it was pointless to enter. However, outside was fair game. And so it was, they decided to wait in the cold morning air until the service was over. It would be then, they reasoned, they would be able to pounce on Jack and anyone else of the male gender who looked healthy enough to man a cannon, hoist a sail, and climb a ship's rigging.

If caught, Jack and other unfortunate souls would be PRESSED into service. Clapped in irons if necessary, then rowed out into the deep water of the Thames Estuary known locally as The Ray where a Man-o-War, a ship of the line, was anchored.

Like many of their kind had done so on previous occasions this Press Gang also took advantage of a lull in proceedings as respite from chasing through streets and muddy lanes. Therefore, to while away the time, like others had before them, they sharpened up their knives and cutlasses on the top of a seventeenth century tomb where lay the mortal remains of one Mary Ellis.

If there was anyone in the church who by then was not aware of the presence of the Press Gang, they soon became so on hearing the sound of metal on stone. Swish swish, swish swish as the gang sharpened their weapons. Swish swish. It was time for Jack and all young men and boys in the congregation to disappear.

As they quickly made their way down the nave to the back of the church near the inner porch door (which the good Rector had carefully closed after his meeting with those waiting outside) the rest of the congregation raised their voices with a particularly rousing hymn to drown the sound of stone upon stone as the Verger and the Rector moved aside a black marble memorial slab to reveal steps to the Clark family burial vault. It was down these steps the men folk and boys ventured to make their timely escape through a tunnel hewn out of the rock concealed behind the wooden remains of lead lined coffins. To the vigorously sung refrains of a normally sedately sung hymn with the Rector and Verger singing with extra loud gusto to make up for the lack of male voices, the marble slab was neatly replaced.

Having been consoled by kindly neighbours Jack's wife Molly and the children arrived at the church just in time to see the doors open and a small assembly of parishioners consisting only of women, their daughters and the old and infirm making their way-out into the cold winter's early morning air.

Wearing a broad smile Molly also witnessed the gang force their way past the Rector and into the church then after considerable time reappear with much swearing and expressions of disappointment and bewilderment on their flushed faces "You look as mad as some say our King is" shouted Molly. "Oh e's mad alright." shouted another while pointing at the Gang "Mad to have these blockheads in his Navy and what with us still at war with o'l Boney e' must be bloody barmy. This lot came up here looking for what exactly?"

The sound of mocking laughter followed that empty-handed Press Gang all the way down the hill to their rowing boat, if not all the way back out to the Ray.

Jack, Molly and the children were all soon reunited and lived a long and happy life as part of the community of Leigh.

Of cause the marble cap stone has long since been sealed in place leaving the dead to be truly left to rest in peace. And what of the tunnel you may ask. Well, there has always been much speculation as to where it surfaced.

Some believe that it led all the way down the hill to one of the many drinking establishments along Leigh Street. Others are convinced that it led to the Rectory. However, as the teller of this story I know for certain where it led too but, with no intended disrespect to you my reader, for the time being I think I will keep that a secret. And nobody can press me to do otherwise.

As Jack walked down old Leigh Street
A press gang there he chanced to meet
They demanded he should join the fleet
On board a man-o-war, boys
On board a man-o-war.

[The Tomb of Mary Ellis locally known as 'The Cutlass Stone' for reasons described in the story above is located just outside the door of the Tudor Porch of St Clement's Church, Parish Church of Leigh-on-Sea. Essex. The wearing down of the stone and a deep gash is visible above the inscription:

Here lies the body of Mary Ellis,
daughter of Thomas & Lydia Ellis
of this Parish
She was a virgin of virtuous courage
And very promising hope
and died on 3rd of June 1609
aged one hundred and nineteen.]

The Book with No Beginning or End

“What do you think of the house so far” asked the Professor as he opened the old heavy creaking door into the library “It's a little bit scary” replied John. “Yes, I suppose it is” said Professor Frampton as he lit a candle. “But that can be down to how much you allow yourself to be inquisitive enough to stretch your imagination. Here before you, as you can see”, continued the old gentleman “are many books to aid you in such thoughts if you so wish.”

The boy stepped into the dimly lit room that smelt of a bygone age. Apart from where long heavy fraying curtains concealed what might have been French doors, leading out into the windswept darkness, the walls were covered in tall dark wooden shelving housing hordes of musty dusty books.

“You are most welcome to get yourself absorbed into a book while you stay here at the house but never choose and open a book that has no title, for if it has no title it has no beginning and no end. And what is a story without a beginning or an end? Anyway, I'm just popping out. Will you be alright?” “Yes fine” assured John

When the old professor eventually returned to the library the book with no title was on the floor and open at the first page. Slowly the Professor bent down and picked it up and read “Once upon a time there was a boy named John.”

Putting the book back in its place on the shelf the old man chuckled and said, “So now the story has a beginning.” From between the book's leather-bound cover could be heard muffled screams but the old man took no notice, blew out the candle and slowly closed the library door. "I wonder" he muttered to himself as he shuffled down the dark wood panelled corridor "who will be the next disobedient child to open that book with no title and bring the story to an end?"

As the nights started to draw in, I decided to write a 'dark' story for Halloween and here it is.

The Shepherds Tale

The now fast fading year had seen a glorious summer, but the Brent geese had arrived early to their rich eel-grass feeding grounds. It would seem they knew that along the Essex shore line and further afield it was going to be a very long hard cold winter. As fellow storyteller Taffy Thomas would say. "An iron winter."

Those of the small village community of Leigh who had wished for a white Christmas had sadly wished in vain. Nevertheless, although somewhat late for that all-important time of the year, soon those same people would have snow in abundance. For when it eventually came it would lay deep on the saddle-back hill. Smoothly, and silently, it would encase the old ruined castle and thickly cover the flat ice-capped dyke-lined marsh lands below. Those unchanged marshes that stretch far out to embrace Old Father Thames as he slowly flows past and makes his way eastward and then with a gaping mouth drinks in the ice-cold waters of the grey North Sea.

Due to the coming weather conditions having been predicted as severe, and even though there was an R in the month, the small shallow drafted-boats of the village below the hill had already been securely moored and some partially covered with scraps of oiled tarpaulin in anticipation of not, for quite some time to come, being able to sail and venture out into the tidal estuary to enable the crew to manually rake the precious cockle beds.

The shepherds on the Downs being wise old boys also knew a thing or two about nature and the signs and warnings she gives, so they got their sheep under the cover of the barns up at the Colonel's place at Hadleigh Farm before the cold winds blew in from the north.

That was in the morning ahead of the snow which had, at round about teatime, started to fall. It didn't arrive on the wings of a blizzard as expected but for that time being floated down thickly, silently, muffling the very sounds of mother earth herself.

It was already thick on the ground by the time old shepherd Henry discovered he was one sheep short from his flock.

I was told he counted those sheep so many times, just to make sure there indeed was one missing, that once or twice he fell asleep doing so. Anyway, at last having decided that he was one sheep short, wrapped up warm against the bitter cold, he trudged crunching his way back up towards the castle looking for it.

By now the snow had stopped falling. It was dark and old Henry didn't have a light and although he had a torch, batteries weren't included. And although he had a paraffin lamp, he didn't have a match with which to light it.

Slowly he made his way through the darkness and then he stopped, put his hand to his ear and listened. Then out of the stillness of the night came the sound of the sheep bleating. “Baa, Baa.” So, he followed the sound to where the sheep was... stuck in some mud.

Now you my observant reader will be thinking how the sheep got stuck in mud. Surely the ground was winter hard. Well, in my 'neck of the woods' it is well known that if there's mud to be found, a sheep will find it. Yes, up to its belly in snow but still it found some mud. Sometimes stories are like that.

Well, although Henry wasn't the sharpest shearing blade in the pen, he didn't want to get stuck himself, so standing on firm ground he grabbed hold of the sheep's tail and he pulled and he pulled and he pulled. And the sheep went “Baa” and the mud went slurp. And the mud went slurp and the sheep went “Baa” but didn't budge an inch staying firmly stuck there in the mud. So, Henry came over the saddle-back hill and down into the village to fetch his wife who immediately asked him if he wanted a cup of tea. ('im looking cold an' all that). “I ain't got no time for tea” says he “but I would be pleased if you would come an' 'elp pull sheep out the mud.” Being the dutiful wife, she agreed.

So off into the darkness they went together but neither of them had a light, although they had a torch, batteries weren't included and although they had a paraffin lamp, they didn't have a match with which to light it.

So, what did they do? Yes, they put their hands to their ear's and listened. Then out of the stillness of the night came the sound of the sheep bleating “Baa... Baa.”

So, they followed the sound to where the sheep was… stuck in the mud. Well Henry himself didn't want to get stuck. So, standing on firm ground he grabbed hold of the sheep's tail and he said “Wife. You 'old on to me and we'll pull together.” And they pulled and they pulled and they pulled and they pulled. And the sheep went “baa” and the mud went slurp. And the mud went slurp and the sheep went “baa” but didn't budge an inch and stayed firmly stuck, there in the mud. So, Henry asked his wife to fetch their daughter. So, the wife came over the saddle-back hill and down into the village to fetch their daughter who wasn't too pleased to be asked to help pull a sheep out of the mud because she was all made up ready to meet a blind date down the street in the Crooked Billet Pubic House. She had been really excited about it all week but had told no one especially members of her family

However, being the good daughter she was, she agreed to help to pull the sheep out of the mud. So off into the darkness they went, mother and daughter, together but neither of them had a light. They had a torch, but batteries weren't included and although they had a paraffin lamp, they didn't have a match with which to light it.

So, what did they do? Yes, they put their hands to their ear's and listened. Then out of the stillness of the night came the sound of the sheep bleating "Baa... Baa."

So, they followed the sound to where the sheep was... stuck in the mud. Well, as you will remember Henry also didn't want to get stuck in the mud. So, standing on firm ground he grabbed hold of the sheep's tail and said "Wife. You 'old on to me. Daughter. you 'old on to your mother and we'll pull together." And they pulled and they pulled and they pulled and they pulled and the sheep went "Baa" and the mud went slurp. And the mud went slurp and the sheep went "Baa" but didn't budge an inch and stayed firmly stuck there in the mud. So old Henry asked his daughter to fetch her brother. So, the daughter came over the saddle-back hill and down into the village to fetch her brother who wasn't too pleased because he was also about to go on a blind date at the Crooked Billet and had been really excited about it all week but like his sister, he had told no one (especially members of his family).

However, being the good son he was, he agreed to help pull the sheep out of the mud. So off into the darkness they went, sister and brother together, but neither of them had a light. They had a torch, but batteries weren't included and although they had a paraffin lamp, they didn't have a match with which to light it.

So, what did they do? Yes, they put their hands to their ear's and listened. Then out of the stillness of the night came the sound of the sheep bleating "Baa, Baa."

So, they followed the sound to where the sheep was... stuck in the mud. Well, Henry the Shepherd, not wanting to get stuck in the mud himself (especially in front of his whole family) stood, on firm ground and grabbing hold of the sheep's tail he said "Wife you 'old on to me.

Daughter you 'old on to your mother. Son you 'old on to your sister and we'll all pull together." And they pulled and they pulled and they pulled and they pulled and the sheep went "baa" and the mud went slurp. And the mud went slurp and the sheep went "baa", and do you know what? The bloody sheep's tail came off in the Shepherd's hand. And I'll tell you another thing. If that sheep's tail had been stronger then this tale would have been longer.

I haven't got the faintest idea as to where I might have first heard or read the like of this story. If at all. All I know is that I have been telling it for years, especially in schools with a small alteration to a particular word just before the end.

Alone

Sooty household chimney smoke battled for prominence against the unrelenting thickening grey early evening fog that swirled like a gigantic serpent's tail engulfing the gas- lit Edwardian streets.

At number 7 Pantile Mews, a large stone three storied family house and home of the Barber family of three, while struggling yet again to make a decent job of tying his bowtie Mr Barber called out for his wife Diane to assist. “Damn thing” he muttered under his breath as Diane entered the bedroom. “You would think” Diane said jokingly “after all these years of your business dinners and all the other social gatherings we attend you would be able to dress yourself.” “I would like to meet the person who invented these things. I'd give him bowtie; I'd tie it tight around his neck and strangle him with the wretched thing” her husband replied in a huff.

Taking the strip of white material from her agitated spouse Diane examined it and frowned. “Look at the state of it. It's all creased and wrinkled. Where's the other one? You can't wear this.” she said. Then after a pause still frowning, she continued “I do wish you wouldn't say such nasty things about people. Such words and thoughts can have a habit of rebounding in one way or another” “Poppycock” her husband retorted. “Complete and utter nonsense.”

Lucy, their young daughter, peered round the bedroom door. “Mummy, Daddy, is Mrs Claydon coming over while you are out?” she asked “No not tonight darling. Mr Claydon is not too well so Mrs Claydon is going to stay at home to look after him. And just as well on a night like this. But you will be alright. You are a big girl now" replied her mother. Lucy ventured further into the room as her father went to the wardrobe drawer. There he took out a small pristine green oblong box with gold insignia, in which was another tie he had purchased in an expensive store along the Brompton Road.

Sitting on the bed Lucy watched her mother expertly wrap the length of white silken fabric around her father's starched winged collar and tie it into a neat stylish bow befitting a gentleman about town.

Mr Barber looked at himself in the dressing table mirror and admired his wife's creativity, kissed her on the cheek and put on his swallow-tailed evening jacket. Turning to Lucy he said, "Pass your mother the clothes brush please darling". "I'll do it daddy." his daughter hastily replied. And standing on the bed trying her hardest not to wobble on top of the luxuriously soft mattress she vigorously brushed her father down. "Careful" her father laughingly exclaimed "You will brush me completely away at that rate." "Finished" said Lucy then toppled over and was engulfed in the sweet-smelling quilt covered eiderdown.

Giving his daughter a tickle and a kiss then another tickle for good measure Mr Barber instructed that when he and Lucy's mother left the house, Lucy was to put another coal on the fire and leaving the hall oil lamp burning she was to put out the one on the landing and then go straight to bed.

"Come on dear or else we are going to be late. We mustn't keep Sir Aston waiting" said Diane over her shoulder as she made her way down the palatial curved marble staircase; her evening gown creating a light swishing sound against the ornate brass balusters.

The Barbers were certainly not poor, nor were they overly rich compared to many in their social circle.

However, it's safe to say they were quite comfortably well off and enjoyed such things in life that you my valued eager reader, maybe like me, could possibly only dream of.

Mr Barber, leaving the bedroom followed his wife down the stairs into the entrance hall and donning a fashionable cape and silk topper he then lovingly wrapped a long woollen lined velvet cloak about the shoulders of his spouse as protection from the cold, damp, night air.

Lucy having finally untangled herself from the soft plentiful bedcovers now stood on the landing leaning over the banister rail holding up the discarded crumpled bowtie "What shall I do with this?" she enquired. "Perhaps it will suit one of those many dolls you have accumulated over the years that take up half your bedroom" replied Lucy's mother with a smile "I do wish you would get rid of them now you are older. Some of them are so worn and ugly they give me the creeps. Now come down stairs and say goodnight."

Lucy did indeed come down but not in what one might call the conventional manner. Hitching up her dress she gave the brass banister rail a polish with her lace trimmed drawers and petticoats as she speedily slid down to the inlaid patterned marble hallway floor and went over to a small child's rocking chair in a dimly lit draughty corner of the spacious entrance hall. There she placed the crumpled tie around the neck of an old cracked glaze-faced china doll that seemed to have occupied that same space forever; well certainly as long as Lucy could remember. In fact, on reflection if the truth be known; who it was that first brought the doll into the house, nobody seemed to know. It was just always there!

Lucy's unorthodox entry into the hall had not gone unnoticed. "Naughty children meet a grisly end" warned her father with a grin "Darling," said his wife quietly "this is not the time or place to put such thoughts into such a young mind." "I was only joking" he replied as he gave his daughter a hug. “Right then Lucy” he said “Give me and your mother a kiss goodnight and remember what we said. Put a coal on the fire, deal with the lamps and then straight to bed. Its late enough now as it is. Oh, and make sure the door is firmly shut behind us. We have a key. See you at breakfast”

Lucy gave both parents a kiss then watched them step out into the darkness of the night with its creeping swirling fog into which they were engulfed and soon disappeared from view. Lucy then waited behind the door which she held half ajar listening to the sounds of their walking and conversation reverberating from off the tall affluent dwellings lining the damp pavement of the South Kensington street until eventually such sounds ceased somewhere in the far distance.

Leaning her back against the red painted front door with its polished knocker on which hung a ripe berried holly wreath the young girl firmly pushed it shut in the face of the murky outside world. Then after a moment's hesitation she slightly, so very slightly reopened it to assure herself there was nobody lurking behind the lone evergreen bush that grew against the iron railings marking the perimeter of the property.

On the chill air came the sound of carolling and a dog sporadically barking. Lucy again closed the door, double checking it was securely shut then went to the lattice leaded widows either side to make sure the catches were secure and then drew a weighty velvet drape across each of the casements. Gingerly she ventured into the darkened parlour and as instructed, put a coal on the fire. As she did so the flames reared up like demons from the underworld and cast elongated shadows like arms across the room as if to ensnare her and drag her down deep into the infernos of hell.

Lucy screamed and ran out, slamming the door behind her; the sound of which echoed through the house as while trembling and as white as a winding-sheet she turned the key firmly in the heavy metal rim lock.

I take pause here in my tale to request you my reader to be sympathetic by casting your mind back to when young. And in so doing, remember what it was like to be left on your own. Because it was then, if like me you had a vivid imagination, your thoughts started to work overtime and quite often, not in a pleasing way. In your mind's eye you saw things that weren't there, and your hearing deceived you into thinking the slightest sound was that of a fiendish creature standing behind you and about to devour you whole.

Back in the hall Lucy rushed around frantically closing and locking all the doors to adjoining rooms then climbed the stairs as fast as her legs would carry her. It was when she had barely reached the top that there was a knock on the front door and a few blood red holly berries fell to the step and rolled onto the path. Lucy froze. She felt her heart pounding at an alarming rate as she stood there on the top tread beneath the pale glimmer of the solitary wall mounted landing lamp.

There came again a determined knocking at the door and more berries fell. Lucy wanted to scream; to cry out "Go away leave me alone" but no sound left her lips for her mouth was, through fear, as dry as brittle parchment. Then to the accompanying strains of a concertina and fiddle came the sound of voices singing. "Silent night, holy night. All is calm all is bright." When at last the rendition of this popular carol ended there was another knock on the door followed by shouts of "Joys of the season and a Merry Christmas." Leaving the door, with its wreath now quite berryless, the small amateur band of happy carolling Waits departed and Lucy now with mellow thoughts of joy and happiness tentatively took down the lamp, turned down the wick and blew out the flame then went to her room where she lit a candle and prepared for bed.

First she closed the wooden shutters over the fastened windows. Then across those she pulled together two heavy embroidered curtains. Humming the tune of the past carol she undressed and donned her hand stitched white cotton nightdress.

After using the commode, she went to the marble-topped wrought iron washstand supporting a pink floral designed bowl with matching water pitcher. There she wet flannelled her hands and face. Then, having dried herself on the dainty hand towel from off the side rail, sitting in front of the bevelled edged mirror she leisurely brushed out her long blond hair. Stroke by long, long stroke. Then suddenly she stopped. Gazing across the room behind her, depicted in the mirror's reflection, she viewed her doll collection neatly displayed on shelves with others below heaped higgledy-piggledy on an old well-worn wobbly French wicker straw backed chair. “Had those on the chair moved of their own accord?” she questioned quietly to herself. “Of course not” she said out loud. “How could they, they are only dolls. They must have just slipped on that particular unstable piece of bedroom furniture”

To set her mind at rest she got up, went to the chair and straightened the faulty leg; then looking up at the shelves she immediately had the notion that none of dolls were in the same places as she had viewed them a moment before when looking in the mirror. “Don't be silly Lucy, you are a big girl now” she reassured herself. Had not her mummy told her so that very same evening! “Yes, I'm a big girl now” Lucy repeated the words over and over again and added “I'm being childish and silly.” But then she thought, what if someone was there, there in the bedroom, her bedroom, hiding and silently moving things about.

Cautiously she edged open the wardrobe door and looked in There was nothing there except her clothes but then "SNAP" a hanger broke and Lucy shrieked as a garment fell to the bottom of the closet then spilled out over the floor and her naked feet. She cried out again, as like treading in slippery slimy treacle, she anxiously tried to step away clear from the loose silken fabric. Having eventually done so she leapt into bed and hid under the covers. Laying there in the silence as she tried to justify her stupidity, she felt sure she could hear her own heart beating like a bandsman's bass drum on Horse Guards.

Eventually she cautiously peeked out from below the white cotton sheets then quietly leaned over the edge of the bed and looked underneath and saw nothing but her holiday trunk and a number of well-thumbed travel books. Laying back on the soft, warm cosy eider duck down pillow she relaxed and willed herself to conjure in her mind pleasant thoughts of staying with her great aunt Phoebe on Sark and the long sunny summer days frolicking in the wind high on the blue wild flowered cliffs. The boat trips to the rocky coves. The wooded valleys and the whole general atmosphere of peacefulness and safety. This done she snuffed out the candle and slowly, gently drifted into the hazy borderlands of being half awake and half asleep.

Suddenly with a start she was alerted by the sound of a quick clickety-click, clickety-click from downstairs in the hall as the occupant of the child's rocking chair stood up on tiny stiff-toed feet and mounted the stairs while chanting in a squeaky voice…

"Lucy, Lucy are you there.
China doll has left the chair.
Lucy, Lucy be aware.
China doll now on the stair."

Lucy let out a petrified scream as she jumped out of bed and ran to her bedroom door to lock it. But, in her terrified haste she fumbled with the key and in the darkness, it dropped to the floor. Crying with fear, she went down on all fours frantically searching for that small iron instrument of her possible deliverance from the fiendish being approaching her bedroom door.

"Lucy, Lucy be aware
China Doll has left the stair.
I'm on the landing
I know you're there."

All at once the whole room resounded with wicked laughter from the dolls on the shelf as they jumped down to the floor. Demonic laughter also came from the collection of dolls that had been laying higgledy-piggledy on the broken chair and where now in the darkness of that room disentangling themselves and making their way across the small Persian rug towards their horrified owner.

Lucy scrambled back into bed and brought the covers tight over her head to block out the terrifying sights and sounds. There she lay sobbing and trembling. Then all of a sudden, the laughter ceased. All went quiet and eventually Lucy chanced to peep from beneath her sweat damp sheets. As her sight adjusted through the dimness, she could make out that nothing was displaced and with a certain amount of confidence restored she reached out and relit the candle.

Yes, all the dolls were in their place on the shelf and the others laying higgledy-piggledy on the broken chair. Yet again young Lucy rebuked herself for being so silly. "It was nothing more than a bad dream. A nightmare" she sighed. "Just a childish nightmare." Lucy then went to the wardrobe and re-hung the silk garment on a new hanger then from the draw she took two clean sheets and re-laid her bed. Having puffed up and rearranged the pillow Lucy once more settled down to sleep and as she did so she heard a squeaky voice say... “That's nice Lucy now we are alone.”

Opening her eyes wide Lucy screamed on seeing, in the flickering light from the candles flame, the face of the china doll but only a breath's distance from her own holding in its hands the white creased and crumbled bow tie which it put around the young girl's neck.

As the doll pulled the strip of white material tighter and tighter and poor Lucy wildly kicked and thrashed struggling for air that cracked glazed-face assailant repeated the much-used expression of the time “Naughty children meet a grisly end.”

I'm told (if others are to be believed) it was but only a few minutes later that Lucy's parents arrived home.

Unknowingly squashing the fallen blood red holly berries under foot Mr Barber opened the front door quietly so as not to awaken their daughter. “I'll just take a peek at Lucy to see she's alright before we also turn in for the night” said her mother as she ascended the stairs. Crossing the landing towards Lucy's room she saw iridescent candle light through the gap beneath the closed door. Very slowly turning the brass knob handle she opened it and looked in. There lay her beautiful daughter, her only child, peacefully still. She gently stroked and kissed the young girl's brow and feeling it to be cold she straightened out the dishevelled bedcovers and pulled them up to cover her daughter's shoulders. Suddenly Lucy screamed and sat bolt upright firmly clutching hold of her mother.

“Mummy, Mummy” she sobbed as tears streaked her face which looked distinctly mottled in the flickering candlelight, “Don't leave me alone again” pleaded the poor child, “Please, please I beg you, don't leave me alone. You won't will you? Promise me you won't.”

“No, we won't” reassured her mother as her father entered the room. “Had a bad dream have you Lucy? A nightmare?” said her father. “No Daddy it was no dream” replied Lucy and between bouts of hysterical crying she went on and tried to explain what had happened. She described her dolls moving and laughing and the china doll coming up the stairs but at that point her father cut her story short “Yes” he said tenderly “It's very late. We are both here now, so you lay down and go back to sleep. It was just a bad dream that was all, just a bad dream. It will be forgotten by the morning. Now, if you would like to give me the bowtie you are wearing, I will take it down stairs and put it back on the china doll where I thought you had left it. I think it gives the old doll an air of elegance and in turn adds a certain something to that draughty corner of the hall. Why you then decided to wear it to bed I don't know and anyway you are wearing it far too tight. You could have been strangled.” Lucy's mother glared at her husband.

Lucy reached up and felt the tie about her neck, and instantly her face turned an ashen grey; as grey as the thick fog still surrounding number 7 Pantile Mews.

There are many variations of the two normally short stories 'Alone' and 'China Doll'.

One Halloween many years ago I was telling stories for the National Trust at Claydon House in Buckinghamshire when I decided to combine my two versions of those two stories as one and here is my written version of that amalgamation.

The ending, you the reader I'm sure will realise is optional in its telling.

Uncle Bertie

Uncle Bertie, the family magician,
was a sizeable part of our Christmas tradition.
With a swish of his cloak, a magic word;
silence, then a cooing heard
as from his hat he conjured a dove
To remind us that Christmas was a time of love.
Then a puff of smoke, a flash of light,
The dove is now a rabbit white.
Into the hat by the ears
the rabbit goes, then disappears.
"Uncle, how's it done?" we yell,
"Tell to us your Magic spell."
"Maybe next year" we are always told
as now from his hat his hand takes hold
of silk kerchiefs, first one, then two,
changing colour from red to blue.
Orange, violet and indigo
are the colours next on show,
then canary yellow, then the brightest green
and before our very eyes-Surprise-a rainbow can be seen
as slowly it drifts down to the floor,
disappears and is seen no more.
A volunteer is now needed quick
to assist with Uncle's next magic trick.
With upraised arms for him to see
and loud shouts and screams of "Me, me, me"
we all surge forward, now very persistent
for we all want to be a magician's assistant.
A girl is chosen, we boys complain,
every year it's just the same.

“Hush your noise” we are told
but there’s always one who’s far too bold.
“It's not fair” he will shout
and for his trouble receives a clout
behind the ear
given not with Christmas cheer
from an Aunt, or Uncle within easy reach
always ready for a boy to teach
the Golden Rule, word for word,
'Children should be seen but never heard.'
Uncle Bertie now begins to clean
the sharpened blade of a guillotine
as he explains to his volunteer
there’s nothing at all for her to fear.
With her head now firmly upon the block
“Go wrong?” says Uncle, “What poppycock.”
The glinting blade is pulled up high,
The volunteer begins to cry.
Girls are silly and very weak,
there’s always one who has to shriek
as the blade comes swishing down
while Uncle’s grinning like a clown.
The blade has, it would seem,
sliced through her neck, quick and clean,
but she moves her head from left to right
Without a drop of blood in sight.
A girl will faint, which then results
in using Grandma’s smelling salts.
The show is over, Uncle takes a bow,
leaving us to wonder how
His magic tricks were done so well
and if next year he would really tell
to us his Magic spell.

Another piece of verse from my 1987 radio play
Long Gone Are the Days

On Trial

"I believe you to be a liar, and you live in a world of fantasy, for are you not a storyteller and do you not tell stories for a living?" said the Prosecution. "I am" said the grey whiskered man in the dock "and yes I do."

"There" said the bewigged barrister turning towards the bench "he lives in a world of make believe, he is well practised in the art of deceit. His words can't be trusted. This man is a maker up of stories and so without a doubt a liar. There my Lord and eminent members of the Jury I rest my case."

"If that be so" said the accused "then why did the clerk of this court offer me a Bible on which to swear? For does not the Bible itself contain stories?"

The above story just came to me, popped into my head as I was compiling an assortment of tales I tell for this my first book ***'Tales from The Shore and More'****. I hope you have enjoyed reading the stories as much as I have done writing them.*

A Carol for Leigh

Down by the Strand, down by the shore
A child is born at number four
That's what I heard a cockle man say
Unloading his boat on Christmas Day

Sing you well and be of good mirth
God's bless'ed son is here on earth
'Wassail, wassail to the King of all Kings
Hail, All Hail!' the angels sing

Across snow-dusted furrowed land
Where ice has made the water stand
Shepherds come having left their sheep
On the castle hill so steep.

Chorus

Three foreign men who've come from afar
Eat shrimps, eat cockles and share a jar
With the shepherds they cheerfully greet
On the Strand where so many now meet.

Chorus

In a fisherman's cottage plain and bare
Amongst the nets and cockle rakes there
Mary, young, so meek and so mild
To God gives thanks for her darling child.

Chorus

Come all good people of this town

Rich and poor come gather round
For whoever you may be
A child is born in Leigh-on-Sea

Chorus

In 2006 it was suggested by a member of The Leigh-on-Sea Town Council that I write a carol for their annual Christmas event 'Carols on Strand Wharf'. My contribution 'A Carol for Leigh' places the nativity scene in the Leigh Old Town. The inspiration to make a local setting of the Christmas Story comes from the Medieval Mystery Plays.

Music Scores

The River is Flowing

Sweet Bells

Dream not of Tomorrow

Fisherman's Boy (1)

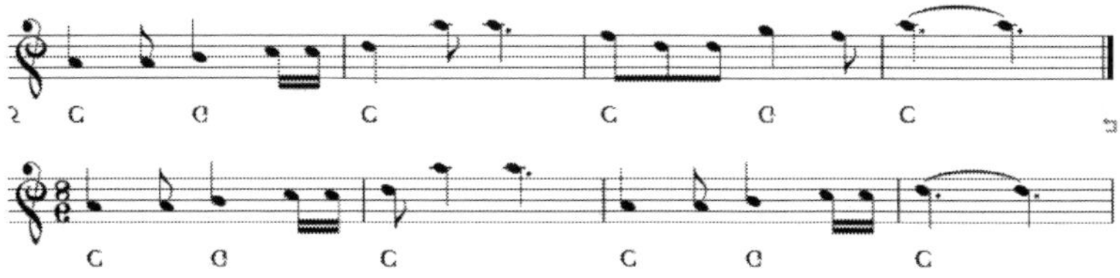

Fisherman's Boy (2)

A Carol for Leigh

The Society for Storytelling is the national organisation that supports both storytellers and the Oral tradition across Britain by promoting their work and building a network for all those in community to use and to share, for at its heart Storytelling is about sharing.

The SfS, run almost entirely by volunteers, has seen a surge in both storytellers becoming members and in the general public's interest in Storytelling. Part of that cycle of growth and informing has to be the researching and collecting of stories before they are lost. These stories can often be a vital part of a community's identity.

Therefore, we are delighted to see this publication of Peter Monk's collection of stories 'Tales from the Shore and More'.

Paul Jackson Chair of the SfS
www.sfs.org.uk